BREATH OF THE SAGES

Ancient Yogic Wisdom for Modern Well-Being

BHOG

INDIA • SINGAPORE • MALAYSIA

ISBN
Paperback 979-8-89556-398-4
Hardcase 979-8-89588-389-1

Table of Contents

Preface

The genesis of this book, "Breath of the Sages: Ancient Yogic Wisdom for Modern Well-Being" a treatise distilled from my personal journeys, crystallized during profound dialogues with my confidants, Mahesh and Mayank. Their unwavering support and sagacious counsel are pillars upon which my resolve to author this volume rests, and for that, they have my deepest gratitude.

The insights within these pages are not revelations unbeknownst to us; rather, they are familiar echoes of wisdom we've encountered through various conduits. My endeavor is to strip away the obfuscation of complex language that often clouds such wisdom, presenting it in a manner that resonates and is easily assimilated—eschewing the labyrinthine prose that can sever us from the very quintessence we seek to grasp. My narrative is steeped in simplicity, reflective of my own understanding and preference for the unadorned truth. The tapestry of this work weaves together the threads of our inherent human nature, our cherished traditions, and the cultural and scientific frameworks that enhance our comprehension of not merely our physical form, but the triad of bodies and quintet of sheaths that constitute our being. These concepts shall be unfurled and examined with meticulous care within the pages to come.

I am but a sojourner on a quest of self-discovery, sifting through the annals of various cultures, gleaning the essence of their wisdom like pollen to create a honey of knowledge for communal benefit. We often construct our lives upon the foundations of prescribed ideologies, canonical texts, and prescribed lifestyles, seldom questioning the underpinnings of such edifices, allowing them to sculpt our Ahamkara—our pride, our identity. In doing so, we inadvertently contravene the primal laws of nature, crafting an edifice of self that segregates us from the collective.

Have we not discerned, at various junctures, the layers of identity foisted upon us? From the moment of birth, we are labeled by species, gender, name, caste, socioeconomic status, and an ever-expanding litany of labels that serve to delineate and distance us from our intrinsic essence. As we traverse life's journey, we amass these identities, progressively estranging ourselves from the core of our existence—a mere speck within the cosmic expanse.

In our pursuit to embellish or sustain these facades, we lose sight of our ephemeral tenure on this terrestrial sphere, neglecting the finite efforts we can render, and the unique endowments granted by nature to serve the collective good.

By this book, my ambition is to dismantle these illusory constructs, liberating us from the shackles of false identities as I have liberated myself. We shall navigate the machinations of the world, understanding how our innate desires are exploited for others' gain, leaving us depleted in body and spirit.

We will revere our bodies, these venerable vessels bestowed by nature, with an exhortation to breathe deeply, to immerse ourselves in the splendor of creation, and to nurture our most primal sanctuary.

Together, we will revisit the ancient Vedic wisdom bequeathed by the noblest of souls to expand our consciousness, enhance our lives, and elevate our service to the world.

This book is not a definitive resolution but a beacon, illuminating a path to perceive reality as it is—a journey through our perceptions (Anubhuti) towards a clearer vision of existence.

Foreword

In a world ceaselessly barreling towards the complex, there emerges a clarion call for simplicity, a beacon guiding us back to the roots of ancient wisdom. "Breath of the Sage Ancient Yogic Wisdom for Modern Well-Being" is not merely a book; it is a vessel carrying the timeless teachings of the sages, a conduit through which the whispered secrets of old are conveyed into the tumult of our contemporary existence.

> The sages of yore spoke of balance, of a harmony between the self and the cosmos, a symphony that has been drowned out by the cacophony of modern life. Within these pages lies a sanctuary where the symphony is restored—note by delicate note—through the hallowed practice of yoga, the very breath of the sages.

Yoga, as you will discover herein, is far more than the postures that have become emblematic of its practice in the West. It is a philosophy, a way of life, a methodical unraveling of the complex tapestry of existence to reveal the serene white cloth of peace lying beneath. This book invites you to partake in this unraveling, to learn how the ancients harnessed the breath to foster an inner garden of well-being.

The author, a diligent scholar of life's symphony, has traversed the valleys and peaks of human experience to distill the essence of yogic wisdom into practical insights. These are not prescriptive teachings but rather guiding principles, meant to be woven into the fabric of daily life. They do not ask you to retreat from the world but to engage with it more fully, with a greater sense of awareness and connection.

As you turn these pages, you will be introduced to the foundational principles of yoga—beyond the asanas—to the breath that animates all life, to the meditation that stills the waters of the mind, and to the ethical tenets that fortify the soul. You will learn of the sages' view on well-being, a holistic tapestry that interlaces the physical, mental, and spiritual into a cohesive whole.

"Breath of the Sages" is a testament to the potency of ancient wisdom in addressing the ailments of the modern era. It is an invitation to slow down, to breathe deeply, and to invite the tranquil wisdom of the sages into your life. May you find within this book a respite from the unending race of life, a moment of peace in which to contemplate the true meaning of well-being, and a breath that nourishes not just the body, but the spirit as well.

Welcome to a journey that transcends time, to a practice as relevant now as it was millennia ago, to a conversation with the sages that never ceased—it only awaited a listener attuned to its frequency. Welcome to "Breath of the Sages."

Bhog's Backstory

Bhog grew up in a quaint village, where the rustling fields and humble homes were the backdrop to his lower-middle-class life. His father toiled under the sun as a farmer, while his mother managed their modest household. Bhog, with his dreams and aspirations, found companionship in his younger sister Geet.

In the heart of their quaint village, Bhog and his younger sister Geet experienced a childhood filled with boundless imagination and shared adventures. The siblings were inseparable, creating a tapestry of memories that would weave its way through the fabric of their lives.

Their days often began with the radiant warmth of the morning sun, beckoning them to explore the world that unfolded beyond the thresholds of their home. Bhog, a protective elder brother, and Geet, with her eyes shining with curiosity, embarked on countless escapades that transformed the mundane into magical.

One of their favorite pastimes was venturing into the nearby woods, where ancient trees whispered tales of forgotten times. Armed with woven baskets, the siblings would collect colorful wildflowers, pinecones, and any treasures the forest offered. These woodland expeditions became a ritual, a journey into a realm where every rustle of leaves and chirp of birds was a symphony of nature's secrets.

The village river, a shimmering ribbon of liquid silver, held a special allure for the adventurous duo. On hot afternoons, Bhog and Geet would escape the watchful eyes of their parents to dip their toes in the cool, rippling water. Skipping stones across the surface became a friendly competition, each sibling vying for the title of the ultimate stone-skipping champion.

Their home, a haven of laughter and shared dreams, often transformed into a canvas for imaginative play. Blankets draped over furniture became the walls of a makeshift fortress, protecting them from imaginary foes. Pillows were repurposed into daring steeds, carrying them on epic quests through the vast landscapes of their living room.

Geet, with her boundless creativity, would orchestrate whimsical tea parties in the backyard. The siblings, adorned in makeshift crowns and fancy attire, would sit on a checkered blanket, sipping invisible tea from mismatched cups, and engaging in conversations with their stuffed animal guests. These tea parties weren't merely pretend; they were grand affairs filled with laughter, love, and the magic of Geet's imagination.

Their evenings were often spent beneath the star-studded sky, where Bhog would point out constellations and share tales of celestial wonders. Wrapped in blankets, the siblings would lie on the grass, dreaming of far-off galaxies and the adventures that awaited them among the stars.

As Bhog and Geet navigated the tapestry of their shared childhood, they weren't merely siblings; they were co-authors of a story written in laughter, exploration, and the enduring bond that time could never unravel. Their childhood adventures laid the foundation for a lifelong connection, a treasure trove of memories that would anchor them through the currents of time, binding them in a love that transcended the ordinary.

As the years progressed, one warm summer evening, as the golden hues of the setting sun painted the village fields in a warm glow, Bhog found himself working alongside his father in the family's modest farmland. The rhythmic sounds of their tools against the earth created a comforting melody, setting the stage for a profound conversation.

Bhog's father, a weathered yet wise man, looked over at his son with a gaze that carried years of experience and resilience. The air was filled with the earthy aroma of the soil, and the distant sounds of village life provided a serene backdrop to their interaction.

As they worked side by side, Bhog's father began to share stories from his own youth, tales of hardships, triumphs, and the invaluable lessons life had imparted to him. The setting sun cast long shadows, accentuating the lines on his father's face, each one a testament to the challenges he had faced and overcome.

"Life, my son," Bhog's father began, his voice carrying a quiet strength, "is like these fields. It's unpredictable, and the harvest is not always guaranteed. But what you put into the soil, the effort you invest, that's what defines the bounty you reap."

Bhog listened intently, absorbing the wisdom his father offered like the soil soaked in the evening dew. His father continued, weaving lessons into the fabric of their shared labor.

"Patience," he emphasized, "is the key. Just as we wait for the crops to grow, life unfolds at its own pace. Rushing through it only leads to disappointment. Learn to appreciate the process, my son."

The old man paused, wiping the sweat from his brow, and looked at Bhog with a twinkle in his eye. "And remember, every challenge is an opportunity. Just like the weeds that threaten our crops, challenges in life are meant to be faced, not avoided. Confront them, and you'll find strength you never knew you had."

Bhog nodded, his hands still tending to the soil. His father's words resonated deeply, like seeds planted in the fertile ground of his consciousness.

"Respect the land, respect nature," his father continued. "In the same way, respect the people around you. We are all interconnected, and our actions have consequences. Treat others with kindness, and you'll find that kindness returned to you."

As the conversation unfolded, Bhog felt a sense of connection with his father that transcended the physical act of farming. The fields became a canvas for life's lessons, and the bond between father and son grew stronger with every shared moment.

The sun had dipped below the horizon by the time they finished their work, and the sky adorned itself with a tapestry of stars. Bhog's father, with a warm smile, placed a hand on his son's shoulder.

"Remember, Bhog, life's true richness lies not in what you accumulate, but in the relationships, you nurture, the lessons you learn, and the person you become in the process. That, my son, is the harvest that lasts a lifetime."

As they made their way back home, guided by the soft glow of lanterns in the distance, Bhog carried not just the physical fruits of their labor but also the seeds of wisdom sown by his father. The lessons from that evening would become guiding stars in Bhog's journey, illuminating the path toward a life rich in meaning and purpose.

In the heart of the village, Bhog's mother, a pillar of strength and grace, played a pivotal role in fostering harmony within the family and extending that warmth to the community. Her name, Ananya, meaning 'unique' in Sanskrit, perfectly captured the essence of her character.

Ananya's days began with the first light of dawn, as she gracefully moved through the rhythm of household chores. The aroma of freshly baked bread and the sound of pots clinking resonated from her kitchen, becoming a comforting symphony that echoed through the humble dwelling.

Her interactions with the neighbors were akin to a gentle breeze that carried goodwill. Ananya would often exchange pleasantries with Mrs. Sharma, the elderly widow next door, ensuring she had enough to eat and assisting with daily tasks. The aroma of spices wafting from their kitchen mingled with the fragrance of blooming flowers, creating an atmosphere of communal warmth.

Ananya's harmonious behavior extended beyond the confines of her home. When the neighboring children sought refuge in her courtyard during their impromptu games, she greeted them with a smile and a plate of freshly made snacks. Her home became a sanctuary for laughter and camaraderie, a haven where the boundaries between families blurred into a shared sense of community.

Within the family, Ananya's role went beyond the traditional duties of a homemaker. She was the emotional anchor, the soothing presence that turned everyday moments into cherished memories. Bhog and Geet, in their youthful exuberance, often sought solace in their mother's gentle guidance.

Ananya's approach to relatives who had once mocked the family's misfortune was nothing short of remarkable. Rather than responding with bitterness, she greeted them with open arms during village gatherings. Her ability to rise above judgment and maintain dignity left an indelible impression, slowly melting away the icy layers of criticism that had been cast upon the family.

In moments of adversity, Ananya's wisdom shone brightly. When tensions arose with neighbors over trivial matters, she became the peacemaker, effortlessly diffusing conflicts with her soothing words and a genuine willingness to understand the perspectives of others. Her courtyard became a gathering place for shared stories, laughter, and the occasional communal effort of preparing meals during festivals.

The first instance that etched a painful memory in Bhog's heart was when his family lost their inherited land. The once-vibrant gathering of relatives turned into a mockery, as whispers of misfortune echoed through the village. The very people who shared the same bloodline now subjected Bhog's family to taunts and ridicule, leaving an indelible scar on his pride. The family once celebrated as landowners became the target of snide comments and condescending glances from relatives. During a family gathering, a distant uncle openly mocked Bhog's father, insinuating that he had failed as a farmer and a provider. The whispers of gossip echoed through the village, and Bhog could feel the weight of judgment on his young shoulders.

Relatives constantly pressuring and insulting them became a part of their daily existence. The weight of societal judgment and disdain weighed heavily on Bhog's shoulders. However, deep within him, a flicker of determination sparked, a flame that would later fuel his journey to rise above the circumstances.

As Bhog grew older, the pressure from relatives intensified. His aunts and uncles seemed to revel in pointing out the family's shortcomings at every opportunity. They questioned his father's ability to manage the farm and openly criticized his mother for not being able to host lavish events like the more affluent families in the village. Bhog's sister, Geet, often became the target of cruel remarks about her family's social standing at school.

Fueled by the desire to escape this cycle of humiliation, Bhog threw himself into his studies, determined to prove his worth through academic success. He excelled in school, earning scholarships and accolades that momentarily silenced the relatives' judgment. However, the uneasiness lingered, and Bhog knew that true vindication lay beyond the boundaries of academic achievements.

As Bhog embarked on his journey to attain worldly success, Ananya remained a steadfast supporter, reminding him that true fulfillment lay not just in personal achievements but in the connections, he built and the kindness he shared with others. When Bhog faced challenges on his quest, it was his mother's voice echoing in his mind, reminding him of the importance of empathy, compassion,

With a scholarship in hand, Bhog ventured into the city to pursue higher education. Fueled by a desire to prove his worth, Bhog set out on a quest for worldly success. He wanted the expensive car, the fashionable clothes, the luxurious house – all the symbols that society deems as markers of success. With grit and determination, he climbed the ladder of materialistic achievements, driven by the need to silence the voices that had once mocked him.

As Bhog delved deeper into the pursuit of materialistic success, he found himself ensnared in the web of consumerism and societal expectations.

Bhog, in an attempt to showcase his success, bought a flashy and expensive car. The sleek vehicle became a symbol of his achievements, but instead of genuine joy, he found himself constantly worrying about its maintenance and status. The initial thrill of driving a luxury car faded, leaving behind a sense of emptiness as he realized that the car was merely a facade masking deeper insecurities.

Bhog filled his wardrobe with designer clothes, aiming to gain social approval and validation. However, he soon discovered that the more he indulged in fleeting fashion trends, the hollower he felt. The pursuit of constantly staying in vogue became an exhausting cycle, as he realized that true self-worth couldn't be measured by the labels he wore or the trends he followed.

His desire for a grand house led him to invest in a spacious, luxurious home. Yet, as he walked through the empty rooms, the echoes of loneliness resonated. The vastness of the house only emphasized the void within, prompting Bhog to question the true purpose of these extravagant possessions.

Bhog became immersed in the world of social media, meticulously curating an online persona that mirrored his supposed success. Each post was carefully crafted to garner likes and comments, but the fleeting validation provided by virtual interactions left him yearning for more. Behind the curated facade, he grappled with a growing sense of isolation.

Attending high-profile parties and networking events became a regular part of Bhog's life. However, the more he networked, the more he realized the superficial nature of these connections. The laughter and applause at social gatherings only served as a temporary distraction from the underlying dissatisfaction that persisted within.

In each of these instances, Bhog's pursuit of worldly pleasures exposed the fragility of his happiness. The materialistic gains he acquired failed to provide the lasting contentment he sought, leading him to question the very foundation of his aspirations. These weaknesses became catalysts for his spiritual awakening, pushing him towards a more profound understanding of fulfillment beyond the superficial allure of material wealth. As Bhog embarked on his ambitious quest for worldly success, the reaction within his family was a blend of pride, concern, and a deep understanding of the sacrifices that such pursuits often entailed.

His father offered him unwavering support, urging him to chase his dreams while reminding him of the importance of staying connected to his roots. His mother sent him off with homemade snacks and blessings, her eyes reflecting a mix of pride and maternal concern.

Geet, Bhog's younger sister, was a blend of admiration and worry. While she admired her brother's ambition, she couldn't shake the fear of losing the closeness they had shared in their childhood adventures. Nevertheless, she stood by him, promising to be his anchor whenever he needed a reminder of the simplicity of their village life.

The extended family and neighbors had diverse reactions. Some viewed Bhog's journey as a beacon of hope, proof that one could break free from the constraints of their circumstances. Others, however, harbored skepticism, questioning the need for such an arduous pursuit when the village life had its own charm.

As Bhog's successes mounted – the prestigious job, the flashy car, the stylish wardrobe – the family's pride swelled. His achievements became a source of inspiration for the younger generation in the village, sparking conversations about possibilities beyond the traditional paths laid out by their forefathers.

Yet, the shadows of concern deepened within the family. Ananya noticed the subtle changes in Bhog – the furrowed brow, the late-night phone calls, the distant look in his eyes. Sensing the toll that the relentless pursuit of success was taking on him, she wrote heartfelt letters, urging him to find a balance between ambition and inner peace.

One pivotal moment occurred when Bhog, surrounded by the glitzy facade of success, returned home for a brief visit. The family, though overjoyed at his return, noticed the weariness etched on his face. Ananya, in a quiet moment, asked him about the price he was paying for his achievements.

Bhog, confronted by his mother's insightful questions, found himself reflecting on the true meaning of success. In that conversation, surrounded by the familiar sights and sounds of the village, he realized that the quest for worldly pleasures had left him spiritually impoverished.

One day, as he stood on the balcony of his high-rise apartment overlooking the city lights, Bhog felt a profound sense of emptiness. The very success he had chased relentlessly seemed like a fleeting mirage. It was at this moment of existential crisis that Bhog decided to embark on a different quest – a quest for meaning, fulfillment, and spiritual understanding.

Bhog stood at the pinnacle of his career, surrounded by the trappings of success that he had always thought he wanted. Yet, amidst the accolades and the acclaim, he felt an unmistakable void, a sense of unfulfillment that no material achievement could fill. One evening, as he walked home through the bustling streets, the cacophony of the city around him, Bhog found himself inexplicably drawn to the serene glow of a small, ancient temple tucked away in an alley.

Stepping inside, the stark contrast of peace within the temple walls to the chaos outside struck him profoundly. As he sat there, the gentle hum of the devotees' prayers enveloping him, memories of his childhood, the spiritual tales his mother narrated, and the deep, philosophical discussions under the Banyan tree flooded back. It was a moment of epiphany for Bhog; he realized that true contentment and fulfillment lay not in the external success he had been chasing but in reconnecting with his spiritual roots and finding inner peace.

This realization marked the beginning of Bhog's true journey, a quest not for worldly achievements but for spiritual enlightenment and the sharing of ancient wisdom in a modern context. His motivation became clear: to bridge the gap between material success and spiritual fulfillment, guiding others who might also be seeking more meaningful, enlightened paths in their lives.

His journey into spirituality began as Bhog delved into the ancient texts of the Indian Vedic system. His exploration led him to the ancient wisdom of the Vedas, where he found solace in the teachings of Krishna and Buddha. Bhog immersed himself in the profound philosophy of Advaita Vedanta, unraveling the illusions of the material world. Swami Vivekananda's call for self-realization, Osho's insights on consciousness, and Jiddu Krishnamurti's emphasis on questioning everything resonated deeply with him.

As Bhog delved deeper into the spiritual realm, he started questioning the very fabric of society. He saw a world where industries manipulated basic human needs – food, sex, and fear – to exploit innocence and amass wealth. He dissected the illusions of desire that led to the depletion of physical and mental health, unveiling the harsh reality of a society driven by superficial pursuits. Bhog's transformation wasn't just about personal enlightenment; it became a mission to challenge societal norms. He questioned the consumer-driven culture that preyed on human desires, exposing the manipulative tactics used by industries to exploit basic human needs. Bhog's journey, rooted in the pursuit of inner peace, evolved into a larger narrative of societal awakening and the quest for a more meaningful existence.

The family, sensing Bhog's internal struggle, rallied around him. They became his sanctuary, a place where he could rediscover the values that had shaped his childhood. Together, they delved into the teachings of their culture, exploring ancient scriptures and philosophies that offered a perspective on fulfillment beyond material success.

As Bhog embarked on a new quest, one that centered around self-discovery and a deeper understanding of life's purpose, his family stood by him with unwavering support. The village, too, embraced the transformed Bhog, recognizing the wisdom that had blossomed from his journey.

Bhog's journey was not just a personal transformation; it became a mission to awaken others to the illusion of worldly pleasures and the importance of finding true contentment within. Through his newfound understanding, he aimed to dismantle the chains of societal expectations and lead others toward a path of enlightenment and self-discovery.

In the midst of Bhog's spiritual exploration, a pivotal moment occurred during a deep meditation session that would forever alter the course of his journey. One day, as he sat in profound stillness, surrounded by the soft hum of nature and the gentle rustling of leaves, Bhog experienced an extraordinary vision.

In the sanctuary of his meditative space, Bhog found himself enveloped in a surreal energy. The air pulsated with a mysterious force, and an ethereal light bathed the surroundings. As he closed his eyes, the meditation took an unexpected turn.

Suddenly, a mirror appeared before Bhog – a reflection of his own image, fragmented and distorted. The cracks in the mirror seemed to symbolize the fractured nature of his pursuit of worldly pleasures. In this vulnerable moment, he saw the illusions of his desires shattering before him.

As Bhog gazed into the broken mirror, a divine presence emerged. Lord Shiva, adorned with a third eye and wielding a trishul, materialized before him. The atmosphere was charged with a divine energy as Shiva spoke, "Swayam se Aham ko hata de, Shiv mil jayenge," which translated to "Remove the ego from yourself, and you will attain Shiva."

The divine message resonated deep within Bhog's soul. It was a profound revelation urging him to transcend his ego, to break free from the illusions that bound him to the material world. Shiva's trishul symbolized the destruction of falsehood and the purification of the self.

With a newfound clarity, Bhog understood that the pursuit of true enlightenment required the relinquishment of ego-driven desires. The broken mirror reflected not just shattered illusions but also the potential for self-realization and spiritual awakening. That encounter with Shiva became a catalyst for Bhog's transformation, guiding him towards a path of inner peace and self-discovery.

From that moment onward, Bhog embraced a life of simplicity and introspection, seeking the true essence of existence beyond the fleeting attractions of the material realm. The vision of the broken mirror and the divine encounter with Shiva became the cornerstone of his spiritual journey, propelling him toward a profound understanding of the self and the timeless wisdom that lies beyond the illusions of the world.

After years of chasing material success and experiencing a profound spiritual awakening, Bhog made a decisive shift back to his roots, returning to the village where his journey began. In the tranquility of his ancestral home, surrounded by the lush landscapes that once cradled his childhood dreams, Bhog found his true calling. He started giving discourses to the village people, delving deep into the essence of reality, enlightenment, and the truth of human innate nature. Bhog's talks became a beacon of wisdom, drawing from his own life's experiences to illuminate the paths of others. He spoke of transcending material desires to uncover the profound joy and contentment that lies in simplicity and spiritual connectivity. Through his teachings, Bhog aimed to enrich the lives of his fellow villagers, guiding them towards a deeper understanding of themselves and the universe, and how to harness their experiences for a fulfilled life. His journey from the apex of material achievement to the heart of spiritual enlightenment became an inspiring testament to the transformative power of returning to one's roots and sharing the light of wisdom.

Chapter 1

Food Desire and Fear

In the small, peaceful village where Bhog had grown up, the natural beauty of the landscape was a reflection of the simplicity of life. Nestled amidst green fields and a flowing river, the village had always been a source of tranquility for those seeking refuge from the busyness of modern life. This serene environment inspired Bhog to organize a 3-week retreat, a gathering where people from different walks of life could come together to reconnect with themselves, their surroundings, and each other.

The retreat, however, wasn't limited to just the villagers. Word had spread beyond the boundaries of the village, reaching those who had left for the cities in search of opportunity. Among them were Ravi, a teenager full of energy and curiosity; Amara, a creative young woman seeking her purpose in the city; Kartik, a middle-aged man juggling work-life balance; Anika, a wise elder looking for deeper spiritual understanding in her later years; Yash, a restless teenager navigating identity issues; Radha, a nurturing woman focused on relationships and family; Arjun, an elder wrestling with attachment; and the playful children, Kalpana and Maya, full of innocence and wonder.

Each of them, drawn by the idea of finding peace and meaning away from the pressures of their daily lives, made the journey back to Bhog's village to participate in the retreat. Bhog, knowing the diverse challenges and experiences each participant brought with them, had carefully designed the retreat to offer not just spiritual lessons but a space for personal reflection, healing, and connection.

For 21 days, the retreat would serve as a bridge between the simplicity of village life and the complexities of the city. It would be a space where people could learn from ancient wisdom, share their stories, and find clarity in the quiet moments under the shade of the banyan tree. Bhog's vision was not only to teach but to create a community where everyone could support one another on their journey toward self-realization.

This retreat was the beginning of a shared experience that would weave together the lives of these individuals, helping them discover deeper truths about themselves and the world around them. The stage was set, and the retreat was ready to unfold as a transformative experience for everyone involved.

Bhog began weaving a tale that spoke of the ancient journey of humanity — a journey that began with the simplest of organisms, evolving over millions of years. As the fire crackled and the night settled in, Bhog spoke of the three primal forces that had guided the course of human evolution.

"The first force," he began, "is the instinct for **Food** — a fundamental need woven into the very fabric of our being. Our ancestors roamed the earth, foraging for sustenance and learning to cultivate the land. They understood that survival depended on the nourishment that the land provided."

The people nodded in recognition, their minds retracing the footsteps of those who came before them.

Bhog continued, "Then came the force of **Desire** — the instinct for Sex. A powerful drive that ensured the continuation of our lineage. Through the dance of attraction, bonds were formed, and generations unfolded. Desire, a force that echoed through time, urging us to contribute to the great tapestry of life."

The firelight flickered, casting shadows on the faces of the mesmerized people.

"And lastly," Bhog intoned, "we must not forget the force of **Fear** — the instinct that safeguarded our ancestors in a world fraught with dangers. Fear, a guiding companion that allowed them to navigate the treacherous paths, to protect themselves and their kin."

As Bhog's words hung in the air, a young girl named Kalpana spoke up. "But Bhog, are we bound only by these instincts? Is there more to our existence?"

Bhog smiled, acknowledging the curiosity in Kalpana's eyes. "Indeed, my child. While these instincts form the foundation of our journey, we have been granted the gift of consciousness. We can transcend these primal forces and find meaning in relationships, creativity, knowledge, and spirituality. Our identities may be shaped by these instincts, but the richness of our lives extends beyond, into the vast realms of human experience."

Bhog continued, "We are all born as humans, but our journey to this point has been shaped by countless iterations over millions and billions of years, starting from the simplest form of life — bacteria. The genes we carry today are packed with data, accumulated over time, driven by the need to survive, grow, and sustain. When we break it down, it comes down to three fundamental forces: food, sex, and fear. We need food to live, desire (or sex) to continue our lineage, and fear to protect ourselves. It's simple, isn't it? Deep within, our subconscious is programmed by these basic instincts. No matter how many identities we take on, our genes know our innate nature. We're constantly striving toward these three forces. How we pursue them may differ — how much we need versus how much we want varies from person to person. Some are content with just bread, while others crave a lavish feast. In the end, it's these basic drives that guide us."

Kalpana asked "can you please explain all this in more detail so we can understand the broader perspective behind it?"

"Indeed", Bhog said: "Today, if we look at the bigger picture, there are three industries that dominate: the food industry, the desire industry (movies, clothes, cars, jewelry, real estate, etc.), and the health industry (hospitals, medicines, fitness, insurance, etc.). Why do we call them industries? An industry is simply a collection of businesses that produce specific goods or services. These industries thrive because they provide what we believe we need in our daily lives, and they understand our needs and desires better than we do. To make money, they study us — our wants, our fears — and offer us what we need in the most convenient way possible.

The most effective way to do business is to first offer something people might not even know they need at a low cost or for free. Once it becomes part of their identity, the price gradually increases, maximizing profits over time.

If we reflect, our bodies are born from the five elements of the earth, and our needs are simple. Nature provided everything we truly need for survival in abundance, and it did so without discrimination. The earth gives us oxygen, water, earth, fire, and sky freely to all beings, without regard for species, religion, caste, or nationality. Yet, we humans divided these resources based on our self-created identities and boundaries.

Desires, as we've discussed, operate on the simple difference between needs and wants. We may need water to quench our thirst, but we want cocktails, cold drinks, or mojitos. We may need basic fruits, vegetables, and grains to satisfy our hunger, but we crave burgers, pizzas, or other lavish meals that might even require the death of another animal.

Similarly, we need clothes to protect ourselves from the elements, but we desire branded, stylish garments. We need basic transportation, but we want luxury cars or SUVs. We may need a simple home for shelter, but we desire duplexes, villas, or mansions. The list goes on. The question is: did we truly need all this? When did we start believing that more and more possessions were necessary for happiness and satisfaction?"

One guy named Ravi asked "this is the way the world works, how will the world grow, prosper if we don't desire, if we don't extend our needs to wants? Where would we be if our scientists/engineers/ researchers haven't done all the hard work to help us reach here?"

Bhog listened attentively, offering no immediate answers. Instead, he encouraged the people to consider the impact of their desires on the quality of their lives. He posed a fundamental question: 'Did the pursuit of endless wants truly to enhance the limited and precious life they had been given?'

Bhog continued "We need to take a deeper look at what we mean by 'growth.' Does growth really mean inventing and creating things that allow us to use our bodies less, reducing physical effort, and eventually making us lazier? Now, with the rise of artificial intelligence, it's evident that we are moving toward a future where even our mental faculties are used less and less, leaving our minds to grow idle. Haven't we already seen the damage that many of the things we created for our convenience have done to us? Think about the world around us, the advancements we have, and the comforts we enjoy — do they truly improve the quality of our lives, or are they simply a temporary fix that leaves us craving more and more?"

Bhog looked around, sensing the quiet attention of those listening. "When we focus on satisfying our never-ending wants, it's like being hooked on a drug — the more we get, the more we desire. We always want the next thing, the bigger thing, something better, and yet, we are never truly content. Does this really mean a good quality of life, especially in the limited time we have on this earth?"

He paused to let the weight of those words settle before continuing, "The universe provides for our needs in abundance — food, water, air, nature — but we are the ones who have transformed these basic needs into endless wants. Nature gave us everything for free, without discrimination, but we created divisions and boundaries. In doing so, we lost sight of the beauty of simplicity and the harmony that existed when our needs were balanced with what the earth provided freely."

Bhog's voice softened as he gazed at the peaceful landscape. "Look at how we live now. Our constant desire for more has led us to create divisions among ourselves — whether based on material wealth, possessions, or status. These artificial distinctions have obscured the simple truth that we are all part of the same creation, sharing the same resources. But instead of being content with what nature offers us in abundance, we have created a world where insatiable desire rules. The result is not peace or fulfillment, but a constant chase for more, driven by a void that can never be filled."

The firelight flickered, casting shadows across the faces of those gathered, deep in thought. The serene night, with its quiet stars overhead, provided the perfect backdrop for contemplation. The people realized that their choices were not just about material things, but about something deeper — their relationship with nature, with each other, and with themselves.

Bhog's message was clear: The path forward required a conscious choice, one that balanced the simplicity of nature with the complex desires of human life. His words resonated like a quiet yet powerful reminder, urging everyone to reconsider the balance between what they truly needed and the endless cycle of wants they had become trapped in. The journey was far from over, but the direction had become clearer.

Kartik asked" How can we break free from the cycle of desire and constant comparison with others when it comes to material possessions? Can you share your thoughts on distinguishing between wants and needs, and how it contributes to a sense of internal peace and contentment?"

Bhog said, "Let me share an example with you that many of us can relate to. Imagine you've worked hard for years, saved up, and finally bought a house in a nice suburb. It brings you and your family so much happiness, and for a while, you feel accomplished and content. But soon, something changes. You start noticing others who have bigger houses, more land, or who live in more prestigious neighborhoods. Suddenly, the house that once brought you joy now feels incomplete. You begin to think, 'If I had a house like that, then I would really be happy.'

So, you pour all your efforts, time, and energy into upgrading your lifestyle. You save more, work longer hours, and make sacrifices with the goal of one day buying that bigger house in a fancier neighborhood. After years of striving, you finally achieve that goal. You buy the house. And yes, for a brief moment, there's happiness. But how long does that feeling last? In no time, you find yourself looking at even bigger houses, in even more affluent areas. And once again, the cycle of desire begins, and the satisfaction you once felt disappears.

This isn't just about houses — it applies to everything around us. Whether it's a new car, the latest phone, more expensive clothes, or even our relationships, we are constantly chasing the next best thing. We desire something, work hard to get it, feel satisfied for a moment, but soon, that satisfaction fades, and we start wanting something else. It's a never-ending cycle, and the problem is that we never allow ourselves to feel truly content with what we have.

Now, imagine if, before buying anything, we paused and wrote down what we actually need. If we could distinguish between what's essential for us and what's merely a desire born out of comparison or societal pressure, we would make decisions based on needs, not wants. Then, once we've fulfilled those needs, we could allow ourselves to be genuinely satisfied, without constantly comparing ourselves to others — whether it's our neighbors, relatives, or celebrities.

Think about the peace that would bring. Instead of being trapped in an endless race for more, we'd find freedom in knowing that we already have enough. When we stop chasing endless desires and start recognizing the difference between needs and wants, a tremendous weight is lifted off our shoulders. We no longer carry the burden of constantly trying to keep up, and our minds and bodies feel lighter. The sense of internal peace and calm that comes with this realization is far more valuable than any material possession could ever be."

Food Industry

Earlier when Bhog was navigating the city's diverse culinary landscape, he couldn't help but notice the pervasive influence of the food industry on people's choices. Advertisements bombarded the streets, enticing consumers with visual delights and emotional appeals. The aroma of sizzling, indulgent dishes wafted through the air, creating an atmosphere of constant craving.

Bhog observed how the industry skillfully employed strategies to influence consumer choices. The use of celebrities, enticing claims of healthiness, and visually appealing portions all played a role in shaping desires that seemed insatiable. As he delved deeper into the intricacies of the food industry, Bhog couldn't ignore the ethical concerns and hidden practices behind the scenes.

His contemplation extended beyond personal desires to a broader perspective on the impact of food choices on the environment, animals, and overall well-being. The stories of factory farming, overcrowded conditions, and the ethical dilemmas surrounding dairy production struck a chord within Bhog's conscience.

As Bhog grappled with the realization that the food industry often played a role in negative karmas, he began to question the identities people created around their food choices. The labels of "foodie" or the cravings dictated by societal norms seemed to overshadow the simple act of nourishing the body.

In his quest for understanding, Bhog also explored the concerns surrounding genetically modified organisms, pesticide residues, and the potential influence of the food industry on dietary guidelines. The intricacies of political lobbying and the shaping of regulations for profit rather than public health weighed heavily on his mind.

Bhog's journey became a personal exploration of breaking free from the false identities tied to food. He sought to encourage others to reevaluate their compulsions and reconnect with the innate wisdom of the brain (Buddhi) rather than succumbing to the desires of the mind (Manas).

Addressing the people the next day of retreat, Bhog shared his research findings with a genuine concern for the well-being of the community. He said "Dear fellow people, I've spent considerable time delving into the intricacies of the food industry and its impact on our choices and health. What I've discovered is both enlightening and concerning, and I believe it's crucial for us to be aware of these aspects that directly influence our lives.

"We really need to rethink our relationship with food and reassess how much of our eating is based on genuine need versus cravings born from our identities. Many of us proudly call ourselves 'foodies' and eat for pleasure, taste, or simply out of habit. But what if we shifted our focus? Instead of choosing food for its taste, we could start selecting it for its nutritional value, understanding that food's primary role is to nourish our body and mind.

When we drop our identity related to food and begin to eat mindfully — choosing what's best for our health instead of indulging cravings — we start to experience real hunger, not the false hunger created by our mind's desires. How often do you feel hungry just because it's a certain time of day? Or because you saw something that looked appetizing? These aren't true signals of hunger; they are cravings formed by habit and identity.

This is where the mind, or Manas, plays a powerful role. Our Manas creates these desires based on the identities we've built around food — whether it's calling ourselves 'foodies' or simply craving certain foods out of habit or social cues. But the truth is, if we let our Buddhi (our intellect) take control, it knows exactly when we need food, how much food is necessary, and what type of food will best serve our health. The Buddhi operates with wisdom, but it often gets overruled by the mind, which seeks sensory pleasures.

Our challenge, then, is to keep our mind clear of these habitual cravings, these 'hacks' from the Manas that push us toward food for pleasure rather than nutrition. By freeing ourselves from this constant cycle of food desires, we can trust our Buddhi to guide us toward healthier choices. Over time, we will learn to eat not just to satisfy a craving or fit a certain identity, but to truly nourish our body and maintain a healthy balance in life.

The food industry, through clever advertising strategies, often entices us with emotional appeals, captivating visuals, and compelling stories. These tactics create cravings for foods high in sugar, salt, and fat, leading us to make choices that might not be in our best interest. They link their products to positive emotions like joy and celebration, making us associate certain foods with happiness.

Celebrities and influencers play a role in this game, endorsing products that may not align with their actual consumption habits. Claims of 'low-fat,' 'low-sugar,' or 'natural' on labels might be misleading, as these products may still contain ingredients that are not entirely healthy. Symbols like hearts or terms like 'organic' can create a false sense of healthiness.

Visual tricks in advertisements can make portion sizes seem larger than they are, contributing to overconsumption. Animated characters and mascots target our children, fostering brand loyalty from a young age. Tie-ins with popular shows and movies leverage characters' appeal, making our children more likely to request specific products.

Moreover, there are concerns about genetically modified ingredients without clear labeling. While debates about GMOs continue, we must strive for transparency in labeling. Pesticides in conventional farming practices might leave residues on our fruits and vegetables, and we may not always be fully informed about the pesticides in our food. Factory farming practices raise ethical concerns about animal welfare and the quality of meat and dairy products.

Our dietary guidelines and food policies may be influenced by the financial interests of the food industry, potentially prioritizing profits over our health. Political lobbying further shapes regulations in their favor.

In light of all this, my fellow people, let us come together to make informed choices. Let us support initiatives for clearer labeling, transparency in farming practices, and regulations that prioritize our health over industry profits. Knowledge is power, and as a community, we can create a culture of mindful and health-conscious living. Let us embark on this journey together for a healthier and happier community.

In conventional or industrial farming, broiler chickens are often raised in crowded conditions in enclosed facilities. Overcrowding can lead to stress, aggression among birds, and difficulties in expressing natural behaviors, as they may not have sufficient space to move and engage in natural activities. Selective breeding for rapid growth is common in the broiler industry.

Chickens are bred to grow at an unnaturally fast pace, reaching market weight in just a few weeks. This rapid growth often results in significant health problems for the birds, such as skeletal deformities, heart issues, and respiratory problems. Many of these chickens suffer from lameness, unable to even walk properly because their bodies can't keep up with the weight they're forced to gain.

Beyond the physical toll, these chickens are typically confined indoors, deprived of natural light and the ability to engage in their instinctive behaviors like dust bathing or foraging. To manage aggressive pecking, which occurs in crowded conditions, the practice of beak trimming (or debeaking) is often employed. This painful process removes part of their beak, impacting their ability to eat and drink normally. When it comes time for transportation, the conditions are harsh and stressful, and many chickens suffer injuries during handling. Even at the point of slaughter, improper methods can lead to further suffering.

We do all of this for the sake of a specific taste, driven by a false identity we've created in our minds around food. By supporting this cycle of exploitation, are we not accruing negative karma? Or do we simply close our eyes and indulge in chicken dishes without thinking of the suffering involved?

Chickens are just one example, but this mistreatment extends to all animals that are weaker and unable to defend themselves. Why don't we see crocodile or tiger meat on restaurant menus as often? It's because those animals are powerful and difficult to exploit, yet we continue to hunt even these creatures to feed our identity-driven desires for strength and pride.

Is it not time to reflect on these choices, to recognize that our actions carry karmic weight, and that we can break this cycle by choosing compassion over indulgence? It's time to consider the lives of the animals we consume and the pain behind our plates, and perhaps, to find new ways of nourishing ourselves that align with empathy and balance.

Similarly, the Dairy Industry today faces grave concerns. While cows have long been revered in certain cultures as mothers and gods, beloved for their nurturing nature toward humans, the demands of modern dairy production tell a different story. Dairy cows are often separated from their calves shortly after birth, causing emotional distress to both the mother and the calf. Male calves are typically sold for veal or beef, while the females are raised to join the cycle of milk production.

In many conventional dairy operations, cows are confined to limited spaces, often indoors or in feedlots, with little room to move. This overcrowding leads to stress and prevents them from expressing natural behaviors, like grazing freely or socializing in herds. Artificial insemination is a common practice to control breeding, and while it may not seem cruel at first glance, its repeated use can add to the overall stress and unnatural conditions these cows endure.

Procedures like dehorning and disbudding are implemented to prevent injuries, but they often cause pain and distress, especially when done without adequate anesthesia or pain relief. Mechanical milking machines, widely used in large-scale dairy operations, also pose risks. Poor maintenance or overuse of these machines can cause discomfort and health issues for the cows. Although some farms uphold higher standards of care — offering regular veterinary attention and humane handling — these practices are often overshadowed by the pressure to maximize milk production.

Selective breeding for higher milk yields puts an immense strain on dairy cows, leading to health problems such as lameness, mastitis (udder infections), and metabolic disorders. The overuse of antibiotics in dairy farming has also raised concerns, particularly regarding the development of antibiotic-resistant bacteria. When a cow is no longer economically viable, she may be sent to slaughter, and the treatment during transport or slaughter often compounds the suffering she endures throughout her life.

Does it truly feel right to consume milk and dairy products from cows that have been mistreated, overworked, underfed, and whose calves are taken away or even killed? Can we honestly believe we are getting the best nutrients from milk that comes from such agony and suffering?

Why do we fail to understand that the meat of chickens or the milk from cows subjected to such pain carries the imprint of their suffering? When we consume these products, we are ingesting not just food, but the energy of distress and anguish. Over time, this will only manifest in physical and mental challenges for us. The misery inflicted on these animals has a way of coming back to us, affecting our health and well-being in ways we may not immediately see but will inevitably experience.

We really need to rethink and break our compulsions tied to our false identities (regarding food) and just try to eat what our body really needs and let our brain do the decision making rather than our mind (Manas)."

Hearing this, the group fell into thoughtful silence. Ravi, always quick to act on what he learned, was the first to speak. "I never really thought about where my food came from," he said, looking down at the simple meal in front of him. "I just ate whatever was there."

Amara, who had always been sensitive to the world around her, nodded in agreement. "In the city, it's easy to forget. Everything is packaged and sold without any connection to the source."

Kartik, juggling the pressures of work and family, had never given much thought to his eating habits beyond convenience. But Bhog's words struck a chord. "I always thought I didn't have the time to think about these things. But now, I realize it's not just about time — it's about values," he reflected.

Even Anika, who had lived a long and thoughtful life, found herself reconsidering her choices. "We have a responsibility to live in harmony with all beings. Perhaps it's time to make a change, even at this stage of my life," she said softly.

Together, the group made a collective decision. They would refrain from consuming chicken and dairy, not out of a sense of deprivation but as a conscious choice to live in alignment with the values Bhog had shared. They would embrace alternate eating habits, exploring plant-based options that not only nourished their bodies but also respected the lives of animals and the balance of the earth.

The shift wasn't without its challenges, but the retreat provided the perfect environment to experiment with new foods and recipes. Radha, with her nurturing spirit, took the lead in preparing meals using local vegetables, grains, and plant-based alternatives. The children, Kalpana and Maya, were curious and excited to try new things, bringing a sense of adventure to the kitchen.

As the days passed, the participants found that their new eating habits brought a sense of lightness — not just physically but emotionally and spiritually. They felt more connected to the earth and more mindful of the choices they made each day.

Desire Industry

Next day when the morning session started, Ravi asked" Bhog, our lives have been entangled in this never-ending pursuit for more – more possessions, more status. How can we break free from this cycle to find genuine peace and contentment in our lives?"

Standing before the people, Bhog imparted his teachings on the pitfalls of succumbing to the Desire Industry and its impact on our lives. He expressed:

"Ravi, in a world inundated with the relentless cadence of desire-driven industries, where every corner whispers promises of happiness in the form of extravagant possessions and societal benchmarks, a thought emerges. I call it the Desire Industry — a realm where needs are eclipsed, replaced by wants, and a new world of aspirations takes root in our minds. We are enticed by idealized standards of beauty, opulent lifestyles, and materialistic benchmarks, each promising a ticket to our elusive pursuit of happiness.

The Desire Industry, with its myriad facets — from fashion and media to the allure of luxury and the gloss of perfection — shapes our perceptions and molds our aspirations. Yet, beneath the veneer of glamor lies a tapestry woven with concerns and criticisms. It fosters unrealistic beauty standards, perpetuates materialism, and triggers a perpetual race for more, as the insatiable appetite of our ego propels us upward on an ever-expanding ladder.

Yet, amid the dazzle of this desire-driven world, a different perspective emerges — a voice that questions the true nature of happiness and the consequences of tethering it to material possessions. How often have we, after acquiring a coveted possession, witnessed the initial euphoria fade into the mundane? The pursuit of happiness, it seems, may be a mirage, as every conquest merely resets the starting point, perpetuating an unending race.

Consider the anxieties that accompany ownership — the fear of losing what was once a source of pride. The expensive car parked at the mall, the luxurious home vulnerable to scratches, and the carefully curated image on social media all become sources of unease, turning the pursuit of joy into a fear-laden journey.

As we dissect the motivations behind our acquisitions, a revelation surfaces. Are we accumulating wealth for genuine personal fulfillment, or is it to showcase our success to the world? Is every possession acquired to meet innate needs, or are they merely elaborate props in the theater of our ego? This introspection unravels the paradox — we accumulate possessions to gain happiness but are often left with the burdensome fear of losing them.

The Desire Industry, in its allure, subtly coerces us into a race, encouraging the acquisition of identities laden with desires and fears. Burdened by loans and societal expectations, we find ourselves on a treadmill, the pursuit of happiness ever-elusive."

Bhog, "but why do we call it a Desire Industry?", One of the kids sitting in front row asked, Bhog responded

"The reason I refer to it as the 'desire industry' is because it manipulates our minds, creating countless desires that overshadow our true needs. It constructs a whole new world of wants that we mistakenly believe are essential to our happiness. For example, they advertise and portray women in such a way that every man begins to dream of these artificial standards of beauty as a necessity rather than a luxury. This constant bombardment of idealized images raises our expectations to unrealistic levels, leading to dissatisfaction in our real-life relationships. We begin to feel that something is missing, which ultimately erodes the harmony in our lives.

Take expensive cars, designer clothes, lavish mansions, and extravagant lifestyles — these are advertised as symbols of success, but instead of seeing them as mere wants, we start to internalize them as needs, believing that obtaining these things will lead to true happiness. This shift towards false desires drives us to work harder, not for personal satisfaction, but to show others how well we're doing compared to them. It becomes a way to elevate our Ego (Ahamkara), separating ourselves from others to feel superior.

But the truth about Ego is that it is insatiable. The more you feed it, the more it demands. Once we fall into this cycle of turning our wants into needs, we find ourselves on an endless ladder, always chasing the next thing that promises fulfillment but never truly satisfies.

Though these industries — fashion, media, entertainment — do contribute to culture and provide artistic expression, there are undeniable negative effects. The fashion industry, for instance, often promotes unattainable standards of beauty through advertising. This can lead to body image issues, low self-esteem, and a constant feeling of inadequacy, especially among young people. Media, including films and television, perpetuate stereotypes and unrealistic expectations about body image, creating a sense of dissatisfaction and negative self-perception in those who consume this content.

By constantly comparing ourselves to these constructed ideals, we set ourselves up for a life of dissatisfaction, forever trying to fulfill desires that never seem to end.

Advertisements often promote consumerism and materialism, encouraging individuals to define their worth by the products they own. This can contribute to overconsumption and a focus on material possessions as indicators of success and happiness. Fast fashion, in particular, has been criticized for promoting disposable and environmentally damaging clothing, fostering a culture of constant consumption.

Some content in films and TV shows may depict violence, explicit content, or situations that can negatively impact mental health, especially when not portrayed responsibly or with proper context. While some people consume pornography without negative consequences, concerns include the potential for addiction, distorted views of relationships, and unrealistic expectations about sex.

Lack of diversity and perpetuation of stereotypes in media can contribute to the reinforcement of biased beliefs and hinder accurate representation of different groups. The underrepresentation of diversity in fashion can reinforce narrow beauty standards, excluding various body types, ethnicities, and identities. Romanticized and unrealistic portrayals of relationships in media can contribute to distorted expectations and potentially impact real-life relationships.

Some argue that explicit content in pornography may shape unrealistic expectations about sex and relationships. Some argue that certain media content, including films and advertisements, may perpetuate harmful values or influence behavior negatively. Debates exist about whether pornography contributes to harmful behaviors, such as objectification, aggression, or unrealistic expectations in intimate relationships. Critics of the porn industry argue that it may contribute to the exploitation of performers, with concerns about consent, working conditions, and the potential for coercion.

This industry gives us false life goals to use materialism as a sure shot way to attain happiness. They are indirectly telling us, buy this car you will be happy, wear these clothes, you will be happy, have a house like this, you will be happy, have a girlfriend/boyfriend who looks this way, you will be happy."

Bhog could see a dilemma in the eyes of the people for this topic being discovered. He tried to explain in a different way. He said, "Let me offer a different perspective," Bhog began thoughtfully. "How often have you experienced this feeling? You dream of buying a new car, watch, mobile phone, or clothes, and when you're about to get it, it feels like a dream come true. But soon after owning it, that initial spark fades, and it becomes just like everything else. I've gone through this countless times in my life. You reach that moment, you enjoy it briefly, but then you're back to where you started. And what do we do? We move the goalpost. We make that new state our ground zero and start chasing the next big thing, always in search of happiness. And what are we left with? An endless race, nothing more.

Why do we buy expensive things, really? Is it for personal satisfaction, to build wealth, or to show the world how well we're doing compared to others? Maybe it's just to meet the personal goals we've set for happiness, whether for ourselves or our families. But have you ever noticed that every such possession brings with it not only a brief burst of happiness but also a new fear — fear of losing it?"

"Let me explain," Bhog continued, leaning forward as the listeners followed closely. "You buy a beautiful, expensive car. You post about it on social media, show it off to your friends, and feel like you're on top of the world when you drive it. You imagine everyone admiring or even envying you. But now, when you park that car, say in front of a mall or on the road, you feel anxious. What if someone scratches it? What if someone bumps into it in traffic? What if the cleaner uses the wrong cloth and leaves marks on the paint? Or if someone steps in and leaves dirt from their shoes? Just look at the number of anxieties you've invited into your life in pursuit of happiness, all driven by your ego.

The very thing that was supposed to bring you joy and fulfillment is now a source of stress and fear. You're no longer at peace because you're constantly worried about losing the thing that was meant to make you happy. And this doesn't just apply to cars. It applies to everything — clothes, watches, mobiles, jewelry, houses, even relationships. We attach ourselves to possessions and people, and the fear of losing them takes hold. So, we keep adding layers of identity to our lives, but with each new identity comes the fear of its loss. Isn't it ironic? We started with simple desires, but we ended up entangled in an endless web of fear and longing.

What's more, many of us, in trying to fulfill these desires, take on loans and burdens. We stretch ourselves financially, thinking these possessions will bring us happiness, but all we end up with is more weight on our shoulders. The simple truth is, the freer we are from unnecessary burdens, the more at peace we feel. Adding weight to our lives — whether through debt or material possessions — doesn't solve anything; it only makes things worse.

I urge you all to reflect on what true happiness really is," Bhog said, his voice calm but firm. "Let's free ourselves from the burden of false desires. True peace lies in simplicity, in being unshackled from the unnecessary weight we place on ourselves in the pursuit of fleeting pleasures. Let's break free from the grasp of the Desire Industry and find contentment in who we are, in what we genuinely need, rather than in what we're told to want."

With these words, Bhog concluded his reflection, urging everyone to look inward and rediscover the simplicity and peace that lie beyond the endless chase of material desires.

Bhog's teachings aim to awaken a sense of mindfulness and simplicity within the people, encouraging them to reconsider their pursuits and find true contentment beyond the illusions presented by the Desire Industry.

Fear Industry

The people, intrigued by Bhog's teachings, gathered eagerly, their faces reflecting curiosity and anticipation. As Bhog spoke, he effortlessly bridged the generational gap, weaving a narrative that appealed to the kids playing nearby and the elders seated under the shade.

Bhog, with a twinkle in his eye, shared anecdotes from his own life, using simple yet profound stories that resonated with the core values of the village. His words were like ripples in a pond, spreading understanding and fostering a sense of unity among the people.

During this gathering, the elders, normally reserved in their interactions, found themselves nodding in agreement with Bhog's wisdom. The children, usually engrossed in their playful activities, listened attentively as Bhog painted vivid pictures of a life guided by simplicity and contentment.

To bring his message to life, Bhog involved the entire community in a collaborative project. Together, they planted a community garden where everyone contributed seeds, nurturing the plants with care and attention. The elders shared their traditional farming knowledge, and the children, with boundless enthusiasm, watered the plants and watched in awe as life unfolded before their eyes.

This shared endeavor became a symbol of unity, care, and love within the village. The garden, with its vibrant colors and diverse plants, stood as a testament to the collective efforts of the people. Bhog's teachings were not just words but a living, breathing reality.

As the sun set on that day, the village echoed with laughter and camaraderie. Bhog, once a lone seeker of truth, now stood surrounded by a community that had embraced his teachings. The elders, children, and everyone in between had found common ground under the banyan tree, fostering a sense of belonging and understanding that transcended the illusions of the Desire Industry.

Next day, Bhog decided to reflect on his third topic of discussion and the most important one" Fear Industry".

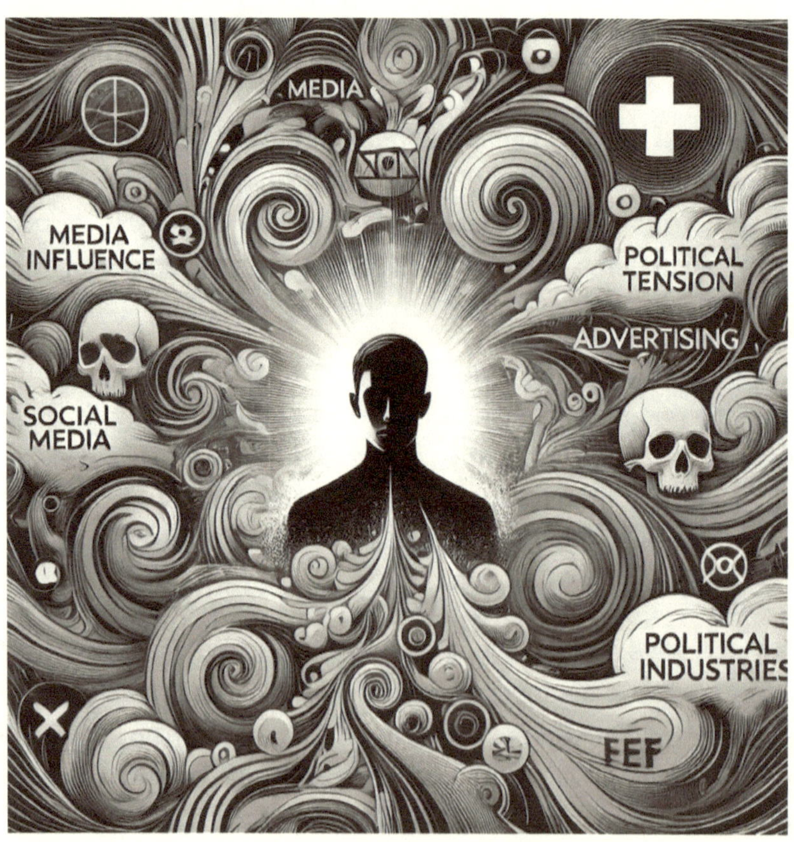

"Fear," Bhog said, "is one of the most powerful forces in human life. It can protect you, but more often than not, it controls you. In today's world, fear has become a commodity, sold and manipulated to keep us trapped. This, my dear friends, is what I call the 'fear industry.' Let me show you how fear is crafted to keep you in its grip."

The group, intrigued, leaned in closer, their faces reflecting the curiosity and anticipation they felt.

"Let's start with the obvious," Bhog began. "**Media sensationalism**. Have you noticed how every day there's a new crisis? Turn on the news, and what do you see? Disasters, violence, threats — constantly. The media thrives on fear because it keeps you watching. Fear is like a hook, and once it's in you, they keep pulling. The more fearful you feel, the more you crave updates, the more you stay glued to the screen."

Kartik, always analytical, nodded in agreement. "It's true. I've found myself unable to look away sometimes, even though it makes me anxious."

Bhog smiled. "Exactly, Kartik. And that anxiety is what keeps you coming back. Fear is addictive, but what's worse is that it blinds you. The more you're immersed in it, the more you begin to see the world as dangerous, and it shapes how you live."

He paused before continuing. "Next, we have something subtler — **social comparison**. It's a fear that most of us don't even recognize as fear. Think about social media. What do you feel when you see someone else's success, their perfect vacation, their ideal family? You start to question yourself, don't you? You fear you're not good enough, that you're missing out, that you're falling behind. This fear of inadequacy — what we call FOMO, or the fear of missing out — is carefully manipulated to keep you constantly chasing."

Amara, who had been reflecting on her own social media habits, spoke up. "It's like I'm always worried I'm not doing enough or that I'm not where I should be."

Bhog nodded. "Precisely. Social media platforms and advertisers play on that fear. They show you images and ideas of 'success' and 'happiness' that make you feel small. And what do they offer as a solution? Products, experiences, things you don't need, but feel pressured to buy because you're afraid of being left out."

The group was silent, each reflecting on how often they had felt that gnawing fear of inadequacy.

"But it doesn't stop there," Bhog continued. "Let's talk about **political rhetoric**. Politicians have long known that fear is a powerful motivator. Fear of the 'other,' fear of change, fear of losing what you hold dear. They use fear to divide you, to make you believe that your safety, your livelihood, even your very way of life is under threat. And when you're afraid, what do you do? You cling to those who promise security, even if it means giving away your freedom, your power, or your ability to think critically."

Yash, who had been listening intently, spoke. "It's like they make you believe that the world is collapsing so you'll support anything they say."

Bhog smiled warmly. "Yes, Yash, and that's the key. When fear takes over, you stop questioning. You accept whatever solution is offered because fear clouds your judgment. And that's the goal — to make you easier to control."

The group exchanged glances, realizing how often fear had guided their actions without them even noticing.

"But let me show you another layer," Bhog continued. "**Economic insecurity**. Fear of the future, fear of losing your job, fear of financial instability. Businesses and markets use this fear to manipulate you into panic-buying, investing in things out of anxiety, or holding onto outdated beliefs about money. How many of you have felt the urge to buy something because you were told that supplies are running out, or prices would go up?"

Ravi raised his hand. "That was me during the pandemic. I bought so much stuff I didn't even need because I was scared it would run out."

Bhog nodded knowingly. "That's the tactic of **scarcity**. Create a sense of urgency, and people will act out of fear. It doesn't matter if the scarcity is real or artificial — what matters is the fear it creates. And it doesn't just apply to goods. Think about **health and safety alerts**. Yes, some warnings are necessary, but often the danger is exaggerated. Pharmaceutical companies, advertisers, and even governments can use fear of illness or injury to push products, services, or even policies."

Amara looked thoughtful. "Like when they overhype certain medical conditions to sell medications?"

"Exactly," Bhog replied. "They prey on your natural desire to stay safe and healthy, but they inflate that desire into fear — fear that you'll get sick, fear that you're not doing enough to protect yourself, fear that you'll miss out on the 'best' solution."

The group sat quietly, the weight of Bhog's words sinking in. Fear was everywhere, it seemed — woven into the very fabric of their lives.

Bhog's tone softened as he continued. "And then there's **technology**. As much as technology helps us, it also breeds fear — fear of being left behind, fear of losing jobs to automation, fear of privacy invasion. Companies and governments use this fear to push agendas, whether it's adopting new systems, investing in certain technologies, or even accepting new surveillance measures. When people are afraid of being replaced, they'll do whatever it takes to stay relevant, even if it means sacrificing their freedom."

Radha frowned. "It's like they make you feel like you have no choice but to follow along."

Bhog nodded solemnly. "Yes, Radha. But that's not all. **Cultural and identity threats** are perhaps the most insidious. Fear that your culture, your traditions, your very sense of self is under attack. This fear is used to pit us against each other, to make us defend our identities in ways that divide us from others. Whether it's fear of immigration, fear of globalization, or fear of social change, this fear makes people cling to old ideas and reject the new, even when the new might be better."

Bhog added "Fear starts in your **Manas**, instills a negative emotion in our mind, which manifests itself as various diseases in our body. Fear triggers the body's stress response, leading to the release of stress hormones such as cortisol and adrenaline. While this response is essential for dealing with immediate threats (the "fight or flight" response), chronic activation can have detrimental effects on health. Prolonged stress, including fear, may suppress the immune system, making individuals more susceptible to infections and illnesses.

Chronic inflammation associated with stress can contribute to various health problems. Fear and chronic stress can contribute to cardiovascular issues. Elevated stress hormones may increase heart rate, blood pressure, and the risk of developing heart-related conditions over time. Persistent fear and stress are linked to mental health issues, including anxiety disorders, depression, and other mood disorders.

Chronic fear can contribute to a state of hypervigilance and heightened arousal, affecting mental well-being. Fear and stress can disrupt sleep patterns, leading to insomnia or poor sleep quality. Lack of adequate sleep, in turn, can negatively impact both mental and physical health. The stress response can affect the digestive system, leading to issues such as indigestion, irritable bowel syndrome (IBS), and other gastrointestinal problems.

Chronic stress may also contribute to inflammation in the gut. Fear and stress often result in increased muscle tension. Chronic muscle tension can lead to pain, headaches, and musculoskeletal issues over time. Persistent fear and stress can impair cognitive function, affecting memory, concentration, and decision-making. Chronic stress has been linked to an increased risk of neurodegenerative diseases over the long term. Fear can disrupt hormonal balance, affecting the endocrine system. This imbalance may contribute to irregular menstrual cycles, reproductive issues, and other hormonal-related problems.

Fear can lead to maladaptive coping behaviors, such as unhealthy eating habits, substance abuse, or avoidance of certain situations. These behaviors can further contribute to health issues. If we remember the covid time and fear mongering done by media channels, the effect of that fear on our stressed minds instills panic and anxiety just to use it against us with the sole intent of making more money. It's by the way not a new thing, fear has been used for a long time by humans/authorities in power to exploit common men."

The group sat in thoughtful silence. It was clear now how deeply fear had infiltrated their lives, shaping their thoughts, actions, and even their sense of self.

Bhog, sensing their reflections, spoke again, this time with a warmth that soothed the weight of the discourse. "Fear is a powerful tool, yes. But it only holds power over you if you allow it to. The 'fear industry' can only thrive if you remain unaware of its tactics. Now that you see how fear is woven into so many parts of your life, you have the choice to break free. Observe the fear, but don't let it control you. Step back, and you'll see it for what it is — an illusion."

Bhog stood, his eyes soft with compassion as he looked at each of them. "Remember this: fear is a shadow. Shine the light of awareness upon it, and it vanishes. The more you recognize these manipulations, the more you reclaim your own power."

Many religious traditions involve a belief in a higher power or deity. Some followers may experience fear related to the divine, which can manifest as fear of divine punishment, judgment, or displeasure. This fear may influence religious practices, moral behavior, and adherence to religious doctrines. Fear of the consequences in the afterlife may shape religious behaviors and adherence to moral codes. Many religions have concepts of sin or moral transgressions. Fear of committing sins and the associated guilt can be powerful motivators for religious adherence. The fear of divine disapproval or punishment for sinful actions can influence moral decision-making."

One elder asked "Bhog, your insights into the interplay between fear and religious beliefs are intriguing. As people seeking spiritual understanding, could you guide us on how we can navigate our beliefs and practices without succumbing to the paralyzing effects of fear? How can we embrace the positive aspects of our faith while avoiding the pitfalls of fear-based influences within our religious communities?

Bhog responded "Dear people, navigating our beliefs and practices within our religious communities while avoiding the paralyzing effects of fear is indeed a thoughtful endeavor. Here are a few guiding principles:

1. **Critical Reflection:** Take time to critically reflect on your beliefs. Questioning and understanding the rationale behind your faith can help you differentiate between teachings that inspire positive growth and those rooted in fear.

2. **Personal Connection:** Cultivate a personal connection with your spirituality. Instead of relying solely on external authorities, explore your inner spiritual journey through practices like meditation, prayer, or contemplation.

3. **Community Engagement:** Engage with your religious community in a spirit of love, understanding, and mutual support. Foster an environment where members can express their doubts and fears openly without judgment.

4. **Education and Awareness:** Seek knowledge about your faith from various sources, not limited to one perspective. This broader understanding can help you discern between genuine spiritual teachings and fear-based manipulation.

5. **Discernment:** Develop discernment to differentiate between healthy religious practices and fear-based control. Trust your intuition, and if something feels oppressive or instills unnecessary fear, question its authenticity.

6. **Supportive Networks:** Connect with like-minded individuals within your community who share a balanced and open-minded approach to spirituality. This support network can help you navigate challenges and find strength in collective wisdom.

7. **Mindful Practices:** Incorporate mindfulness into your spiritual practices. Mindfulness can help you become more aware of fear-based thoughts and emotions, allowing you to respond with wisdom rather than reacting impulsively.

8. **Embrace Love and Compassion:** Focus on the aspects of your faith that promote love, compassion, and understanding. Embrace these values in your interactions with others, fostering a positive and harmonious community.

Remember, the essence of spirituality lies in personal growth, understanding, and the pursuit of inner peace. By approaching your faith with an open heart and a discerning mind, you can navigate the complex terrain of religious beliefs while cultivating a sense of spiritual fulfillment."

He added, "While fear is often discussed in negative terms, some religious traditions also emphasize positive aspects of fear, such as a reverential fear or awe in the presence of the divine. This form of fear can be seen as a sign of respect and humility. In **Buddhism**, the understanding of fear is often approached in the context of overcoming suffering and achieving liberation from the cycle of birth, death, and rebirth (**samsara**). Buddha acknowledges the existence of fear as a fundamental aspect of the human experience, and it offers a path to understand and transcend fear through wisdom, ethical living, and mental training. Buddhism identifies the fundamental fear that underlies human existence, which is the fear of suffering (**dukkha**).

The concept of ignorance (**avidya**) in Buddhism is often seen as the root cause of suffering. Ignorance refers to a lack of understanding of the nature of reality and the interdependent nature of all things. This ignorance gives rise to fear, attachment, and aversion. Buddhism teaches that attachment (**raga**) and aversion (**dvesha**) are key factors contributing to suffering. These attachments and aversions are often rooted in fear – the fear of losing what is pleasant or the fear of encountering what is unpleasant. Buddhism identifies three mental afflictions known as the "three poisons" – ignorance, attachment, and aversion. These poisons are considered the primary causes of suffering and are closely related to fear. An important Buddhist concept is impermanence (**anicca**). Fear often arises from the human tendency to cling to what is perceived as stable or enduring. "

Bhog noticed a lot of young people busy with their mobile phones while in the session. He continued "Today," Bhog began, "we find ourselves using the Internet as an extension of our minds. It has become a tool to ease our lives, offering instant answers and endless streams of information. But in this constant quest for knowledge and connection, we are unknowingly adding fuel to our subconscious minds, leading to increased anxiety and mental unrest."

"Our minds," he continued, "are designed to handle a specific amount of information. Yet, we continually bombard ourselves with data from social media, news feeds, and incessant online searches. When worry grips us, we turn to the Internet seeking solace, but often, we find ourselves entangled in overthinking, restlessness, and a foggy state of mind. Instead of alleviating our fears, this excess of information often amplifies them."

"We must learn to use the Internet consciously," Bhog advised, "just as we should guide our minds (manas) with intention rather than allowing them to control us. We're inhaling too much — too much information, too much entertainment — leaving little room for real-life experiences. This constant digital immersion leads us to exist more in a virtual world than in the tangible reality around us."

He paused, letting his words settle over the attentive faces. The rustling leaves seemed to echo the urgency of his message.

"Fear, in its essence, is necessary for our evolution and survival," Bhog acknowledged. "It alerts us to danger and prompts caution. However, an overdose of fear — or of food and desire — inevitably leads to problems. This overdose occurs when we chase more than what we genuinely need, when wants overshadow necessities."

"The solution lies in adopting a minimalist lifestyle," he suggested. "By collecting and using only what is essential, we create space for peace within our bodies and minds. Minimalism isn't about deprivation; it's about intention — choosing what adds value to our lives and letting go of the excess that weighs us down."

Bhog's gaze swept across the group, his eyes filled with compassion. "Our innate tendency to seek power and security while trying to escape or conquer our fears is deeply embedded in human nature. This drive often manifests in the relentless pursuit of material wealth, social status, or control over others. It's fueled by a primal instinct for self-preservation and a yearning for stability in an unpredictable world."

"But true security doesn't come from external possessions or domination over others," he continued. "It arises from within — from understanding ourselves, acknowledging our fears without letting them rule us, and finding contentment in simplicity."

Amara raised her hand, her voice tinged with reflection. "Bhog, how can we begin to detach from this constant influx of information and desire?"

"Start by setting mindful boundaries," Bhog replied gently. "Allocate specific times for technology use and be intentional about the content you consume. Engage in activities that ground you in the present moment — like walking in nature, practicing meditation, or spending quality time with loved ones without digital distractions."

"Remember," he added, "the goal isn't to reject the modern world but to navigate it with awareness. Use technology as a tool, not a crutch. Let your mind be a master of these tools, not a servant to them."

Ravi, the ever-curious teenager, pondered aloud, “Is it really possible to live minimally in today’s society?”

Bhog smiled warmly. “It’s not only possible but profoundly liberating. Minimalism doesn’t mean stripping away joy or comfort; it means removing the unnecessary so that the necessary can speak. It’s about recognizing what truly brings fulfillment versus what temporarily fills a void.”

“By focusing on our genuine needs rather than endless wants, we reduce the clutter — not just in our homes, but in our minds. This clarity allows us to face our fears without being overwhelmed and to find peace amidst the chaos.

True spiritual growth and enlightenment require a shift in consciousness beyond the pursuit of personal gain or the alleviation of fear. It involves surrendering the ego’s attachments and desires and cultivating a deeper connection with the divine essence that resides within oneself and all of creation.

In many spiritual traditions, the ultimate goal is not merely to attain worldly success or fulfillment of desires but to transcend the cycle of suffering and attain union with the divine. This requires a profound inner transformation characterized by self-awareness, selflessness, compassion, and a deepening of one’s spiritual practice.

While prayers and acts of devotion can be powerful tools for spiritual growth and transformation, they are most effective when performed with sincerity, humility, and an understanding of the true nature of the divine. Instead of seeking power or security from external sources, true spiritual seekers strive to cultivate an inner sense of peace, contentment, and connection with the divine, recognizing that true fulfillment comes from aligning with the divine will and surrendering to the inherent wisdom and compassion of the universe.

The human tendency to pursue power and evade fear often intertwines with spiritual beliefs and practices, shaping individuals' approaches to devotion and prayer. Throughout history, power has been sought as a means of asserting dominance, control, or influence over others and the environment. This drive for power can stem from a variety of sources, including personal ambition, societal pressures, or a fear of vulnerability. Similarly, the avoidance of fear prompts individuals to seek ways to mitigate or overcome their anxieties, whether through external validation, material possessions, or spiritual practices.

Ultimately, genuine spiritual growth requires transcending egoic attachments and aligning with deeper truths beyond the pursuit of power and the avoidance of fear. It entails recognizing the impermanence of external sources of security and fulfillment and embracing the inherent uncertainty and vulnerability of human existence. By relinquishing the illusion of control and surrendering to the flow of life, individuals can cultivate a deeper sense of inner peace, contentment, and spiritual fulfillment, independent of external circumstances or outcomes.

Kabir, the renowned 15th-century Indian mystic and poet, held a perspective on prayer and divine intervention that was deeply rooted in his philosophy of spiritual realization and inner transformation. Kabir's teachings, which are often expressed through his mystical poetry, emphasize the importance of direct personal experience over blind faith and ritualistic practices.

From Kabir's viewpoint, the essence of prayer lies not in asking for external favors or divine intervention, but rather in seeking union with the divine through inner realization and self-awareness. He believed that the ultimate truth resides within each individual and can be realized through sincere spiritual inquiry and introspection.

Kabir frequently criticized the superficiality of religious rituals and external displays of devotion, advocating instead for a deeper, more authentic connection with the divine. He often used metaphorical language to convey profound spiritual truths, urging seekers to look beyond the external trappings of religion and discover the divine presence within themselves.

In Kabir's view, true prayer involves surrendering the ego and opening oneself to the divine presence that permeates all of creation. It is not about asking for material blessings or favors, but rather about cultivating a state of inner receptivity and attunement to the divine will.

For Kabir, the path to spiritual realization is one of inner purification and self-transformation. He emphasized the importance of ethical conduct, humility, and devotion to the divine as essential aspects of the spiritual journey.

In light of a revelation that prayers will not result in divine intervention or assistance, Kabir encouraged individuals to shift their focus from external requests to inner inquiry and self-discovery. He emphasized the importance of cultivating a direct and intimate relationship with the divine through practices such as meditation, self-inquiry, and devotion

Ultimately, Kabir's view on prayer and divine intervention aligns with his broader teachings on the path to spiritual liberation. He encourages seekers to look within themselves for the answers they seek, recognizing that the divine presence is always accessible to those who sincerely seek it with an open heart and mind."

As Bhog concluded his wise words, the people gradually set aside their mobile phones, looking at each other with a newfound awareness. Bhog's insight had struck a chord, and the hum of nature replaced the incessant buzzing of smartphones

Bhog's teachings resonated deeply with each villager, fostering a collective understanding of the importance of balance. The village, once entangled in the web of digital noise, now was determined to thrive in the simplicity of mindful living.

In the evening, as the sun dipped below the horizon, the people gathered to express their gratitude to Bhog. They presented him with a handcrafted memento — a symbol of their commitment to a life anchored in the present moment. The once-distracted people now cherished each sunrise and sunset, grateful for the harmony Bhog had brought to their lives.

With a heart full of contentment, Bhog smiled, knowing that the seeds of awareness he planted had blossomed into a garden of tranquility, where the people found joy in the simplicity of their existence

As the people started to prioritize their real-life experiences over virtual distractions, a tangible transformation unfolded. Children played outdoors, elders shared stories under the ancient banyan tree, and the aroma of home-cooked meals wafted through the air.

Chapter 2

Science of Breathing

Some time back, Bhog, the spiritual seeker, stumbled upon these profound insights during a solitary retreat in a serene mountainous region. As Bhog sat in deep contemplation, surrounded by the tranquil beauty of nature, a realization dawned – the breath, often taken for granted, held the key to unraveling the mysteries of the mind and body.

In the quietude of the mountains, Bhog observed the rhythm of his breath as it synchronized with the gentle breeze rustling through the leaves. It became evident that the breath was not merely an automatic function of survival; it was a dynamic force intimately tied to the ebb and flow of emotions.

Interconnectedness of mental and physical states

As Bhog delved into the contemplation of breath, the interconnectedness of mental and physical states unfolded. The breath mirrored the inner landscape – racing with anger, slowing with sadness, fluttering with joy, and gasping with fear. It became clear that the mind and body operated in unison, responding to both real and imagined scenarios.

The revelation that the brain couldn't differentiate between real and imaginary threats struck Bhog like a lightning bolt. The implications were profound – the body's response to stress, whether rooted in present realities or fabricated fears, carried significant consequences for overall health.

Bhog reflected on the pervasive nature of fear in the modern world, where uncertainties and anxieties were exploited for profit. Movies, a reflection of scripted scenarios, induced genuine emotional responses, further emphasizing the power of the mind to shape the body's reactions.

Returning to the basics of breathing, Bhog recognized its transformative potential. With a simple exercise, Bhog encouraged others to regain control over their breath during moments of negativity. By consciously slowing down the breath, Bhog believed individuals could reverse the physiological effects of stress, anxiety, and anger. This, in turn, sent signals to the brain that all was well, creating a cascade of calming effects on the mind and body.

In the heart of the mountains, Bhog found a powerful tool for self-regulation and inner peace – the breath, a guide to navigating the intricate dance between mind and body. Through this newfound understanding, Bhog embraced the profound simplicity of breath, recognizing it as a gateway to emotional well-being and spiritual growth.

Next day, as the people gathered in the tranquil village, Bhog took center stage beneath the ancient banyan tree. The air was filled with a sense of anticipation as Bhog began to share his profound insights.

"Our breathing," he began, "is not merely an automated mechanism for sustaining life. It is a dynamic force intricately linked to our emotions, our thoughts, and our overall well-being. In times of joy, sorrow, anger, or fear, our breath mirrors the very essence of our existence."

With a calm and measured tone, Bhog continued to unravel the mysteries of the breath. He spoke of the body's subtle responses to the ebb and flow of emotions, explaining how the brain, unable to distinguish between real and imagined threats, reacts to the thoughts in our minds.

"The gravity of this realization is immense," Bhog emphasized. "Our stresses and uncertainties, whether rooted in the past or projected into the future, manifest as real threats in our body's responses. Fear, my friends, is the silent orchestrator of our actions and our overall health."

Bhog began with a simple statement: "If we can learn to control our breathing, we can reverse the impact of negative emotions." His words hung in the air, and the villagers leaned in, intrigued.

Amara, who had been struggling with stress from her work and personal life, raised her hand. "Bhog, I often find myself overwhelmed by emotions. You said breathing can help control them. How does that work?"

Bhog smiled gently. "Ah, Amara, emotions are powerful forces, but they are closely tied to the rhythm of our breath. When you are stressed, your breathing becomes shallow and fast. When you are calm, it slows down. The beautiful thing is that by consciously controlling your breath, you can send signals to your brain that everything is alright, and in turn, your mind will begin to calm."

Bhog demonstrated a simple technique called **belly breathing**, or **deep diaphragmatic breathing**. He placed his hand on his abdomen, slowly inhaling through his nose. The villagers watched as his belly expanded with the breath, and then deflated as he exhaled. The rhythmic rise and fall of his abdomen were mesmerizing.

"You see," Bhog said, "when we breathe deeply from the diaphragm, we activate the body's relaxation response. This is the key to managing emotions."

As Bhog spoke, Ravi, the eager teenager, was listening intently. He had been struggling with anxiety for weeks. The pressure from school, the expectations of his family, and the weight of his own ambitions had been overwhelming. His mind was constantly racing, and his nights were filled with restless sleep.

That evening, after hearing Bhog's teachings on breath, Ravi decided to try the simple technique of belly breathing. He sat alone in his small room, the moonlight casting a soft glow through the window. Placing his hand on his abdomen, Ravi took a deep breath, just as Bhog had shown, feeling his belly rise. He held the breath for a moment before slowly releasing it.

At first, his thoughts still raced, but after a few minutes, something began to shift. The constant buzzing in his mind quieted down, and the tightness in his chest started to loosen. He hadn't realized how tense he had been until that moment of release.

For the first time in weeks, Ravi felt a sense of calm. It was as if the simple act of breathing had created space in his mind — space where there had only been chaos before.

The next morning, Ravi approached Bhog under the banyan tree. "Bhog," he said, "I tried belly breathing last night. It helped. For the first time, I didn't feel so overwhelmed. How does something as simple as breath have such a powerful effect?"

Bhog smiled warmly. "Ravi, the breath is the bridge between the body and the mind. Our ancestors knew this well. When you control your breath, you are controlling the flow of energy in your body. The mind follows the breath, so when your breath is calm, your mind becomes calm too."

Ravi nodded, understanding the connection more deeply now. He realized that his breath was a tool he could use not just for calming his mind, but for navigating the many challenges he faced in life.

As Bhog continued his teachings, he spoke of how the mind cannot always differentiate between real and imaginary threats. "How many times," Bhog asked the villagers, "have you felt your heart race from something that wasn't truly dangerous? Perhaps a frightening thought, a troubling memory, or even a scene from a movie?"

The villagers nodded in agreement, each recalling their own moments of fear over things that were never really there.

Bhog continued, "Our brain reacts the same way to both real and imagined threats. When we overthink a bad scenario, our body reacts as though the threat is real — our breathing changes, our body tenses, and we prepare for fight or flight. The problem is, when we let these imagined fears go on too long, our body suffers. Stress chemicals flood the system, weakening our immune system and wearing us down."

Radha, always the nurturing figure, raised her hand. "Bhog, I've noticed this in myself. When I worry about my children, even though they are safe, my body feels as if something bad is happening. How can I stop this?"

Bhog looked at her with compassion. "Radha, you must practice controlling your breath in these moments. When you notice your thoughts spiraling, pause and focus on your breath. Slow it down, take deep, deliberate inhales, and exhale slowly. By doing this, you send a signal to your brain that all is well. Over time, this practice will help you manage your emotions, reducing the power of imagined fears."

He paused and looked around at the gathered villagers, continuing to explain. "The breath is an intrinsic part of our overall existence, not just for life but for our emotional and physical well-being. We can influence the mind by mastering the breath. Each emotion — anger, joy, fear, anxiety — has its own breathing pattern, but the good news is that we can reverse the effects of negative emotions by controlling the breath."

Anika, the village elder, had listened quietly to Bhog's teachings on breathing. Over the years, she had accumulated many worries — about her family, about her health, about the future. As Bhog spoke, she realized how much of her fear had been fed by her thoughts, and how those fears had affected her body.

That evening, Anika sat outside her small home, the cool night breeze rustling the leaves. She placed her hand gently on her abdomen, just as Bhog had shown them, and began to breathe slowly and deeply.

At first, her mind wandered to her usual concerns, but she gently brought her focus back to her breath. Inhale. Expand the belly. Exhale. Let it soften. The rhythm became a soothing melody, and slowly, the weight of her worries began to lift. It was as if, with each breath, she was releasing years of accumulated tension.

In that quiet moment, Anika felt something she hadn't felt in years: peace. Not the fleeting peace that comes from distraction, but a deeper peace that seemed to rise from within, carried on the gentle waves of her breath.

As Bhog concluded his teachings for the day, he left the villagers with a simple yet powerful message: "Our breath is not just an involuntary act — it is a tool, a bridge, a healer. If we can learn to harness its power, we can transform our lives, our minds, and our hearts. The next time you feel overwhelmed by emotion, turn inward and control your breath. You will find that the storm will pass, and in its place, you will discover calm."

The villagers left the banyan tree with a newfound understanding. They had learned that something as simple as breathing held the key to navigating the complexities of life. And with Bhog's guidance, they were ready to embrace the power of conscious breath, knowing that within each inhale and exhale lay the path to peace.

Basics of Breathing Process

The villagers gathered once again under the shade of the banyan tree, where Bhog sat, his face calm and serene as always. Today, the air was still, and the curiosity of the people was palpable. They had learned much about emotions, energy, and breath in previous discussions, but today Bhog was about to delve into the science of breathing itself — a subject that connected the spiritual with the biological.

Bhog, being a profound reader with deep knowledge of both the body and mind, began the day's teaching with a calm and reassuring tone. "My dear friends," he said, "today we will explore the science of breathing. I will explain it simply, but the depth of its impact on our minds and bodies is vast. Let's start with the basics."

The villagers, young and old, sat in quiet anticipation. Kartik, who was often concerned with his physical health, looked particularly eager to understand the connection between breath and well-being. Amara, too, appeared thoughtful, as she had been recently exploring how her emotions affected her breath and vice versa.

Bhog continued, "Breathing, also known as respiration, is essential for life. It is the process by which our bodies take in oxygen, which we need for every cell to function, and remove carbon dioxide, a waste product of metabolism."

Kartik, the middle-aged father, often felt the strain of his responsibilities in the form of physical aches and shortness of breath. He had noticed, particularly during moments of stress, how his chest would tighten, and his breathing would become rapid and shallow. Until recently, he had not thought much of it. But after hearing Bhog speak about the power of breath, Kartik decided to observe his own patterns.

One evening, after a long day of work, Kartik sat outside his home, feeling the familiar tension build in his chest. This time, instead of ignoring it, he followed Bhog's advice. He placed his hand on his abdomen and began to breathe deeply, focusing on expanding his belly with each inhale and gently releasing the air with each exhale. At first, his breath was uneven, but soon, it fell into a rhythmic pattern.

As his breath deepened, Kartik felt his chest begin to relax. The tension he had carried all day slowly melted away. He realized then how much control he had over his stress, simply by controlling his breath. The experience was eye-opening. Breath, Kartik thought, was not just an automatic function of the body but a tool he could use to manage his emotions and physical well-being.

As Kartik reflected on his newfound understanding, Bhog continued explaining the science behind the process of breathing. "When we inhale," Bhog said, "the diaphragm, which is the muscle separating our chest from the abdomen, contracts and moves downward. This creates more space in the chest cavity, and air is pulled into the lungs. This air contains oxygen, which is absorbed into our bloodstream."

Kalpana, the young girl, raised her hand and asked, "Bhog, how does the air know where to go in our bodies?"

Bhog smiled gently at the innocence of her question. "That's a wonderful question, Kalpana. Inside our lungs are tiny air sacs called alveoli. These sacs are where the magic happens. Oxygen from the air we breathe passes through the walls of these sacs and enters our blood. At the same time, carbon dioxide — waste produced by our body — moves from the blood into the alveoli, so it can be exhaled. This exchange of gases is what keeps us alive."

The villagers listened intently as Bhog spoke of the lungs and their role in sustaining life. Radha, the mother who had often seen her children's breathing change during moments of excitement or stress, asked, "Bhog, you've mentioned before how breathing affects our emotions. Could you explain how that works?"

Bhog nodded and continued. "Yes, Radha. There is a strong connection between our breath and our emotions. When we are calm and relaxed, our breathing is slow and deep. But when we experience emotions like stress, anger, or excitement, our breathing changes — often becoming faster and shallower. This is because our body responds to emotions by adjusting our breathing patterns, preparing us for action in moments of heightened emotion."

Amara had always been a driven and ambitious woman, but lately, her work had been taking a toll on her mental and physical health. She would find herself in meetings, barely able to breathe properly, feeling as if her chest was constricting. Her mind would race, and by the end of the day, she would be exhausted, unable to unwind.

After Bhog's earlier teachings on breath control, Amara had started paying more attention to her breathing patterns. She realized that during stressful moments, her breath became rapid and shallow, centered in her chest. It wasn't until she consciously tried to slow her breathing — taking deep breaths into her belly — that she found relief.

One particularly stressful evening, Amara practiced deep diaphragmatic breathing as Bhog had taught. As she focused on her breath, she felt the tightness in her chest begin to loosen. Her mind, once clouded with stress, started to clear. She learned that she could take control of her breath to take control of her mind.

Bhog continued his lesson, turning now to the regulation of breathing. "Breathing is regulated by the brain, specifically the respiratory center in the medulla oblongata and pons. This part of the brain monitors the levels of oxygen and carbon dioxide in our blood and adjusts our breathing rate to maintain balance. If our body needs more oxygen — like when we exercise — our breathing becomes faster. If we are at rest, our breathing slows down."

Yash, the teenager, who often felt restless and filled with nervous energy, raised his hand. "Bhog, sometimes I feel like my breath just takes over when I'm anxious, and I can't control it. Is there a way to stop that?"

Bhog looked at Yash with understanding. “Yes, Yash. What you are experiencing is the body’s natural ‘fight or flight’ response. When you feel anxious, your body prepares for action by speeding up your breathing. But you can take control of this by practicing conscious breathing. When you feel your breath becoming rapid, focus on slowing it down. Take deep, slow breaths. This will calm your nervous system and bring your mind back to a state of balance.”

Yash had always been an active boy, full of energy, but lately, he had been struggling with anxiety, especially before exams. His heart would race, his breath would quicken, and he would feel a sense of panic that seemed beyond his control. After hearing Bhog’s teachings, Yash decided to try conscious breathing before his next exam.

The morning of the exam, Yash sat quietly at his desk and closed his eyes. He placed his hand on his abdomen and began to breathe deeply, slowly, just as Bhog had taught. Inhale... exhale... his breath became a rhythm that calmed him. When he opened his eyes, the panic was gone. He felt steady, ready to face the challenge ahead.

For the first time, Yash realized that he could take control of his anxiety through something as simple as breath.

As Bhog brought his lesson to a close, he left the villagers with one final thought. “The breath is not just a biological function. It is a bridge between the body and the mind, between the physical and the spiritual. If you can master your breath, you can master your emotions, your thoughts, and even your health. Our ancestors knew this well, and that is why they created powerful practices like pranayama.”

Nirmala, a young woman who has recently faced significant emotional stress due to family conflicts and the overwhelming pressures of daily life. Nirmala, feeling emotionally drained and disconnected, approached Bhog with her query.

"Hey Bhog, lately I've been feeling a constant weight on my chest, as if I can't catch my breath. My mind is restless, and no matter how hard I try to calm myself; I feel trapped in a cycle of stress and anxiety. Is there any way I can regain control of my mind and emotions? I've heard about breathing techniques, but I don't understand how they can help."

Bhog responded: "Nirmala, your question touches on a very important aspect of our existence — our breath. Often, we overlook the simple act of breathing, which is more powerful than we realize. Practices that promote mindfulness and meditation often involve intentional, slow, and deep breathing. Mindful breathing can have a calming effect on the nervous system, promoting a sense of presence and emotional balance.

We can consciously influence our mood by practicing specific breathing techniques. For instance, deep diaphragmatic breathing or 'belly breathing' can help induce a state of relaxation, while focused and deliberate breath control can be used to manage stress and anxiety.

When your breath is shallow and rapid, your mind mirrors that restlessness, but when you deepen your breath and slow it down, your mind follows, calming and centering itself.

Understanding and being mindful of your own breathing patterns can be a valuable tool for emotional regulation. Incorporating practices like deep breathing, meditation, or yoga into your routine can contribute to overall emotional well-being by promoting relaxation and reducing stress."

Bhog smiled warmly at Nirmala, gesturing to the villagers around them, “Let us now breathe together, slowly and intentionally, and experience how even a few mindful breaths can make a difference.”

As the sun dipped below the horizon, casting a warm glow over the village, Bhog concluded with an invitation. “Let us embark on a journey of mindful breathing, my dear people. In the simplicity of each inhale and exhale, we shall find a pathway to peace, resilience, and a harmonious existence.”

Basics of Nadis

Bhog sat in quiet meditation beneath the vast banyan tree. A group of seekers, filled with curiosity and reverence, gathered around him. The tree’s thick roots seem to mirror the spiritual grounding of Bhog himself. The air is cool, and the leaves rustle gently as the seekers, one by one, begin asking questions.

Amara spoke up first. " Bhog, I've heard of this energy within us, but I don't fully grasp how it moves or how we elevate it to the Sahasrara, the Crown Chakra. Could you explain?"

Bhog, with a calm smile, opened his eyes and began to speak. "Ah, Amara, the energy within us is called **prana**, and it flows through subtle energy channels known as **nadis**. Picture these nadis as rivers within your body, not physically visible, but present in your subtle body. There are said to be **72,000 nadis** in total, but only ten are truly significant. As you practice pranayama, meditation, and yoga, these nadis begin to activate, and the energy rises through the chakras — centers of consciousness — from the base of the spine to the crown of the head. When this energy reaches the Sahasrara, we experience enlightenment."

Ravi, sitting to Bhog's right, leaned forward, intrigued. "Bhog, if there are so many nadis, how do we know which ones are the most important? How can we focus our efforts?"

Bhog's voice was soft yet filled with clarity. "Ravi, the three most crucial nadis are the **Sushumna, Ida, and Pingala**. The **Sushumna Nadi** is the central channel, running through the spine from the root chakra, **Muladhara**, to the crown, **Sahasrara**. It is neutral and balanced, and when prana flows freely through Sushumna, the path to higher consciousness opens. This is the path of samadhi, the ultimate union with the divine."

Meera, thoughtful and reflective, asked, "And what about Ida and Pingala, Bhog? How do they contribute to this journey?"

Bhog looked at her with kind eyes. "**Ida** and **Pingala** are the two complementary forces that must be balanced for the **Sushumna** to activate**. Ida** is the lunar, feminine nadi. It is cooling, calming, and connected to your thoughts and emotions. It runs along the left side of the body. Like the Moon, it reflects and nurtures.

Pingala, on the other hand, is the solar, masculine nadi. It is warming, energizing, and governs action and logic. It flows along the right side of the body, representing the fiery energy of the Sun. These two nadis meet at the **Ajna chakra**, the third eye. When they are in balance, the Sushumna is activated, allowing energy to rise."

Ravi, listening intently, asked, "How do we achieve this balance, Bhog? Is it something we can do with breathwork?"

Bhog nodded, his face serene. "Yes, breath is the key, Ravi. Through pranayama, such as **Nadi Shodhana** or alternate nostril breathing, you can balance Ida and Pingala. Breathing in through the left nostril activates Ida, and breathing in through the right nostril activates Pingala. When you breathe evenly, you bring harmony to these opposing energies. And once they are balanced, the prana flows freely through the Sushumna, allowing the **Kundalini energy** — the dormant energy at the base of the spine — to rise."

Amara, fascinated, asked, "Is the rising of the Kundalini a sudden experience? Or is it something gradual?"

Bhog smiled, as though remembering a distant truth. "It is different for everyone, Amara. For most, the awakening of Kundalini is a gradual process. As you continue your practice, the energy rises slowly, passing through each chakra one by one, clearing any blockages along the way. Eventually, it reaches the Sahasrara, the thousand-petaled lotus at the crown of the head, where we experience unity with the cosmos. But this is not something to be forced. It must unfold naturally, through balance, dedication, and patience."

Meera, ever curious, asked, "Bhog, are these nadis connected to our physical body, or do they only exist in the spiritual realm?"

Bhog's voice was soothing yet filled with wisdom. "The nadis are part of the subtle body, Meera. They do not correspond to the physical nerves or veins, but they do affect your mental, emotional, and physical well-being. When the prana flows smoothly through the nadis, you feel centered, energized, and clear-minded. When the flow is blocked, you experience imbalances, both physically and emotionally."

Ravi then asked, "Bhog, you mentioned other nadis beyond Ida, Pingala, and Sushumna. Can you tell us more about them?"

Bhog nodded. "Yes, there are seven others significant nadis, although they are less frequently discussed. **Gandhari Nadi** flows from the left eye to the left foot, carrying psychic energy, while **Hastajihva Nadi** mirrors it on the right side. **Yashasvini Nadi** runs from the right big toe to the left ear, and Pusha Nadi goes from the left big toe to the right ear. These nadis help to balance the body and connect different energy centers."

Bhog paused for a moment, allowing his words to sink in, before continuing. "Then there is **Alambusha Nadi**, which flows from the anus to the mouth, connecting the lower and higher energies. **Kuhu Nadi** runs from the throat to the genitals, and it is significant in tantric practices where sexual energy is sublimated into spiritual energy. Finally, **Shankhini Nadi** flows from the throat to the anus, and it can be activated through certain yogic practices, such as **Ashvini Mudra**, which involves conscious contraction of the muscles at the base of the spine."

Amara, intrigued, asked, "Bhog, is it dangerous to awaken the Kundalini? Some say it can be overwhelming."

Bhog's expression was gentle, yet firm. "Kundalini awakening is not dangerous, Amara, but it must be approached with great care and respect. If one is unprepared, the rapid rise of energy can lead to physical and emotional imbalances. But when the body and mind are prepared through yoga, pranayama, and meditation, the journey becomes safe, transformative, and deeply enriching. The guidance of a teacher is essential in this process."

Ravi, looking thoughtful, asked one final question. "Bhog, how do we know when we are ready for this awakening?"

Bhog's smile deepened. "You will know, Ravi, when your mind is calm, your breath is steady, and your heart is open. The Kundalini does not rise through force — it rises when you are ready. When Ida and Pingala are balanced, the Sushumna opens, and the energy flows naturally. Trust in your practice, and let the journey unfold in its own time."

The seekers sat in quiet reflection, the gentle breeze carrying Bhog's words deep into their hearts. Under the shelter of the great banyan tree, they felt the stirrings of something ancient and profound within them, a connection to the vast rivers of energy flowing quietly through their being.

Next day, under the timeless banyan tree, Bhog's seekers had gathered once again, the peaceful atmosphere drawing them into deeper reflection. After their previous discussion about energy channels and the flow of prana, Amara had brought up another question, shifting the conversation towards the workings of the body and mind. The sun had moved lower in the sky, casting longer shadows, while the cool breeze carried the scent of earth and leaves.

Amara had spoken softly, her voice filled with curiosity. "Bhog, last time we spoke about the flow of energy and balance within the body, but I've been thinking about how the body relaxes. I've heard of the parasympathetic nervous system. Could you explain how it works and why it's important?"

Bhog had smiled gently at Amara's question, his wisdom flowing as naturally as the wind through the banyan leaves. "Ah, yes, Amara. The **parasympathetic nervous system** is a key part of how the body maintains balance. It is one of two main branches of the **autonomic nervous system**. While the **sympathetic nervous system** prepares the body for action with what is called the 'fight or flight' response, the parasympathetic system serves the opposite purpose — it helps the body to relax, recover, and restore itself. We call this the 'rest and digest' state."

Ida Nadi and Parasympathetic Nervous System

Meera had leaned forward, intrigued by the new concept. "So, Bhog, what happens to the body when the parasympathetic system is active?"

Bhog had nodded at Meera, his voice calm and clear. "When the parasympathetic system is engaged, the body begins to slow down. Your heart rate decreases, your muscles relax, and your digestive system is stimulated to process food more efficiently. It also constricts the pupils and allows the body to conserve energy, promoting a state of relaxation and recovery. This is the body's natural way of restoring balance after periods of stress or activity."

Ravi, always eager to dive deeper into understanding, had asked, "How does it interact with our breathing and other bodily functions? I'm trying to connect how yoga and pranayama tie into this."

Bhog had smiled knowingly, seeing the connections Ravi was beginning to make. "The parasympathetic system plays a crucial role in slowing your breathing, Ravi. When it is active, your breathing becomes deeper and more controlled. This is why, in yogic practices, we focus so much on breathwork. For example, when you practice **Nadi Shodhana** or alternate nostril breathing, you are working to balance the flow of prana through the Ida and Pingala nadis. Breathing through the left nostril specifically stimulates the Ida Nadi, which is connected to the parasympathetic system and the cooling, calming energy it promotes."

Amara had tilted her head, thinking for a moment. "So, breathing through the left nostril activates the parasympathetic system, and that helps us relax?"

Bhog nodded, his expression calm. "Exactly, Amara. The left nostril is associated with the Ida Nadi, which channels the lunar, calming energy. When you engage in pranayama, such as breathing through the left nostril, you directly activate the parasympathetic system, bringing about a sense of relaxation and tranquility in the body and mind. This is why such breathing techniques are often used to calm the mind before meditation or sleep."

Meera had asked another question, her voice filled with quiet concern. "What happens if this system becomes imbalanced, Bhog? Can the Ida Nadi, or the parasympathetic system, be too weak or too strong?"

Bhog's gaze had shifted slightly, as if recalling ancient wisdom. "Yes, Meera, an imbalance in the Ida Nadi or the parasympathetic system can manifest in various ways. When the Ida is weak, it can lead to issues like difficulty in relaxing, emotional numbness, a lack of creativity, or even physical symptoms like coldness in the body. Such imbalances can affect your digestion and sleep, making it difficult to find peace."

Ravi had asked with curiosity, "And when it's overactive?"

Bhog had continued, his tone steady. "When the Ida Nadi is overactive, it can lead to an overwhelming flood of emotions, heightened sensitivity, and difficulty focusing on tasks. You might feel disconnected from practical reality, lost in excessive daydreaming, or face digestive imbalances due to the cooling energy overwhelming the system. The key is balance — too little or too much activation of this energy channel can disturb the harmony within."

Amara, reflecting on Bhog's words, had then asked, "Bhog, how can we restore balance if we feel these symptoms?"

Bhog had smiled, his voice warm. "Restoring balance requires awareness and gentle practice. For an underactive Ida Nadi, you can engage in calming practices like alternate nostril breathing, focusing more on the left side. Gentle yoga asanas, especially twists and movements that engage the left side of the body, can help. Meditation is also important, focusing on calming the mind and balancing emotions."

He had paused before continuing. "And if the Ida is overactive, grounding techniques become essential. Cooling pranayama like **Sheetali or Sheetkari**, which cools the breath, can help. Grounding poses like **Tadasana** (Mountain Pose) and **Balasana** (Child's Pose) are effective for restoring a sense of stability. Remember, the key is to listen to your body and understand the signals it gives you."

Pingala Nadi and Sympathetic Nervous System

Ravi had nodded slowly, beginning to see how the concepts fit together. "So, these practices help us balance not only the Ida and Pingala nadis, but also the sympathetic and parasympathetic systems?"

Bhog had given a soft, approving smile. "Yes, Ravi, exactly. The Ida Nadi and the parasympathetic system work together to calm and relax the body, while the Pingala Nadi and the sympathetic system energize and prepare us for action. Through yoga, pranayama, and meditation, we aim to bring balance to both these energy channels and systems, ensuring that neither is too dominant. This balance is crucial for our overall well-being and spiritual development."

The seekers had fallen into a peaceful silence after Bhog's explanation, each of them reflecting on how the balance of breath, energy, and the body's nervous systems affected their lives. The banyan tree had seemed to whisper its own ancient wisdom as the shadows grew longer. The banyan tree's long branches swayed gently in the late afternoon breeze as the seekers gathered for another session with Bhog. Their previous discussions had left them curious about the deeper workings of Ida and Pingala, but now the conversation was shifting toward specific aspects of the energies they hadn't touched on yet.

Amara, sitting cross-legged, spoke next, her voice thoughtful. "Bhog, you mentioned that Pingala represents solar energy and the power of Rajas, but how does this affect our emotions? You said overly emotional people have high Ida, but what does that mean for Pingala?"

Bhog nodded, taking in her question. "Indeed, Amara. Ida is associated with the emotional, mental aspects, while Pingala represents activity and ambition, but this does not mean Pingala is emotionless. When Pingala is overactive, emotions don't disappear — they are simply expressed differently. Instead of feeling and reflecting, as Ida does, Pingala turns those emotions into action, often in ways that are impulsive or driven by ego. It can lead to hyperactivity, constant movement, or aggressive behavior. Think of the energy as fire — it doesn't stop to reflect but burns brightly, sometimes uncontrollably."

Ravi, his brows furrowed in thought, asked, "Bhog, if Pingala is connected to the fire element and ambition, how does it affect digestion? You mentioned something about the stomach and digestion being linked to Pingala energy."

Bhog smiled, appreciating Ravi's curiosity. "Ah, yes, the stomach, or more specifically, Jatharagni, the digestive fire, is a representation of Pingala's energy in the body. Just as the Sun powers all life, Pingala powers the body's ability to digest food. When Pingala is strong and balanced, digestion is smooth, and energy flows easily. But if Pingala is overactive, it can lead to issues like acidity or inflammation, a result of excess heat. On the other hand, when Pingala is weak, digestion slows down, leading to lethargy or a feeling of heaviness."

Meera, intrigued by the idea of balance between energies, asked, "Bhog, how does Pingala lead us through the chakras? You mentioned it can take us to Vishuddha, the throat chakra. What happens once we reach that point?"

Bhog's face softened as he explained. "Yes, Meera, Pingala takes us up the pathway of action, ambition, and courage. The highest expression of Pingala is the **Vishuddha chakra**, the center of truth and courage. At this stage, you gain the ability to speak the truth and stand up for what is right. It is not just ambition for material success but for living with integrity. However, beyond Vishuddha, the journey becomes more subtle, and this is where Ida comes into play. While Pingala gets you to a place of action and expression, Ida, with its connection to intuition and emotional wisdom, helps you move beyond the physical into the spiritual realms."

Amara spoke again, curious about the balance between the two energies. "Bhog, you said that Pingala can become overactive and lead to things like isolation or arguments. But what about people who feel overly passive or lack ambition? Could this be a sign of weak Pingala energy?"

Bhog looked at her with a gentle smile. "Yes, Amara. When Pingala is weak, a person may feel lethargic, stuck, or unable to take action. They may struggle to make decisions or lack the drive to pursue their goals. This is because Pingala governs our ambition, courage, and the will to move forward. Without that fire, there's no motivation to act. In such cases, practices like **Suryabhedi pranayama**, which activates the Pingala nadi by breathing through the right nostril, can help reignite that inner fire and bring balance."

Ravi, reflecting on the broader implications of Bhog's teachings, asked, "Bhog, you said that many people live their lives stuck at the level of Mooladhara or Swadishtana, focused on basic needs or pleasure. How does strengthening Pingala help us move beyond these lower chakras?"

Bhog's expression grew serious as he answered. "Ravi, most people remain focused on survival and pleasure — this is the reality **of Mooladhara** and **Swadishtana.** But once Pingala is balanced and strong, it allows you to move beyond these base needs, toward **Manipura**, the solar plexus, where ambition and personal power reside. From there, you can continue upward, toward **Vishuddha**, where the highest truth and courage are realized. This progression is key to spiritual growth, but it requires balance with Ida. Too much Pingala will keep you chasing worldly goals; too much Ida will leave you dreaming without action. The balance between the two lets you rise above."

Meera, always seeking practical solutions, asked, "And Bhog, what about when Pingala becomes too strong, leading to things like arrogance or indulgence? How can we bring it back into balance?"

Bhog's voice was soft, yet clear. "When Pingala becomes overactive, Meera, it manifests in arrogance, excessive ambition, or even indulgence in physical pleasures — sex, gambling, addictions. To balance this, one must engage in calming practices. **Nadi Shodhana** pranayama is one such method, alternating the breath between the nostrils to bring equilibrium. Additionally, focusing on grounding asanas like **Tadasana** and **Balasana** can help. If Pingala is overactive, the cooling practices of Ida — such as breathing through the left nostril — can bring balance back."

The seekers sat quietly for a moment, reflecting on the intricate balance of energies that governed their lives. The banyan tree swayed gently in the breeze, its deep roots and strong branches reflecting the grounded yet expansive wisdom that Bhog imparted to them, guiding them toward balance and spiritual growth.

As the sun continues its descent, casting long shadows from the banyan tree, Bhog prepares to give his closing statement. The villagers are now fully engaged, having absorbed the earlier discussion on the balance of energies. Bhog, with a calm and clear voice, begins to summarize the teachings.

Bhog stood, his gaze sweeping over the gathered crowd. “So, in summary, my dear friends, there are three main energy channels in our body, though you cannot see them like you can see your arms or legs. These channels — Ida, Pingala, and Sushumna — represent different aspects of our being. They are like rivers, carrying energy from our most basic instincts all the way to higher wisdom. The left channel, Ida, governs the mind, our thoughts, emotions, and calmness. It helps us relax and find peace within ourselves. The right channel, Pingala, is the energy of action, ambition, and the ego. It pushes us to achieve and get things done, but when out of balance, it can lead to pride, recklessness, and indulgence in harmful behaviors.”

He paused for a moment, letting the weight of his words sink in before continuing. “Balance between these energies is essential. Too much Ida can lead to overthinking, addictions, and emotional instability. Too much Pingala can lead to arrogance, aggression, and a life driven by ego and desires. But when balanced, these energies guide us through life’s journey — helping us rise above basic needs and desires, so we can reach higher consciousness and peace.”

Dance of Energies through Chakras and its effects

Bhog with a gentle smile. “And how do we achieve this balance? Through simple practices, such as Nadi Shodhana — breathing through alternate nostrils to balance these energies. Through yoga, meditation, and mindful living. And remember, each day is a chance to practice — whether the sun shines brightly or the moon brings its cool light, both energies must be in harmony for us to live fully.”

With that, Bhog sat back down under the banyan tree, the villagers deep in thought, reflecting on the wisdom they had just received.

Amara, always seeking balance in life, continues her earlier inquiry. "Bhog, thank you for explaining the relationship between ambition and creativity. But sometimes, I feel like I'm stuck in one energy — either I'm too ambitious and lose touch with my emotions, or I become too reflective and don't take action. How can I find a steady flow between the two?"

Bhog smiled at her, recognizing her internal struggle. "Amara, this is the dance of energies within us — Ida and Pingala, reflection and action. You feel the pull between them because both energies are essential, but they must be in balance. When you focus too much on ambition, you may block the Svadhishthana chakra, which governs creativity and emotions. And when you become too introspective, you may weaken Manipura, which gives you the strength to act. A good practice for balancing these two is Nadi Shodhana, alternate nostril breathing. It harmonizes the flow of energy between Ida and Pingala, allowing your creativity and ambition to work together in harmony."

Amara nodded, feeling relieved to have a practical tool to help her. "Thank you, Bhog. I will practice it."

Next, Kartik, the middle-aged father with many responsibilities, spoke up. "Bhog, my life is filled with duties — work, family, and responsibilities. Sometimes, I feel overwhelmed and exhausted, like my energy is drained. Is this connected to my chakras?"

Bhog turned to Kartik, his gaze compassionate. "Kartik, the exhaustion you feel may be due to an imbalance in your Manipura chakra, which governs your personal power and vitality. When you carry too many burdens without taking time to replenish yourself, you can burn out. Additionally, your root chakra, Muladhara, may be affected. This chakra represents stability and grounding, and when it is weakened, you may feel drained and unsupported."

Kartik sighed, resonating with Bhog's words. "That's exactly how I feel — like I'm carrying too much."

Bhog nodded. "To restore balance, it's important to take time to reconnect with your inner self. Meditation, grounding practices like walking barefoot on the earth, and yoga asanas that strengthen your core will help re-energize you. You must also remember to delegate and release some control; you cannot carry everything on your own shoulders. By nurturing yourself, you strengthen both Manipura and Muladhara."

Yash, the young teenager, who had been listening quietly, hesitated before speaking. "Bhog, I've noticed that sometimes I feel pressure to be someone I'm not. It's confusing — everyone has expectations of me, but I don't always know what I want. How do I know what's right for me?"

Bhog looked at Yash kindly, understanding the struggles of youth. "Yash, at your age, it's natural to feel pulled in different directions. The pressure you feel is often the result of an imbalance in the Ajna chakra — the third eye, the center of wisdom and intuition. When this chakra is not fully developed, we become confused by the noise of others' expectations and lose connection with our own inner voice."

Yash leaned in, intrigued. "So, how do I connect with my intuition, Bhog?"

Bhog smiled. "By practicing stillness, Yash. Meditation is key to opening the Ajna chakra. When you meditate, you calm the mind and allow your inner wisdom to speak. It's also important to trust yourself. When you feel doubt or confusion, pause, breathe, and ask yourself what you truly want. Over time, you will strengthen your Ajna, and your decisions will become clearer and more aligned with your true self."

Anika, the elder in the group, then raised her hand. " Bhog, I have lived many years and experienced much. Lately, I've felt the call to detach from worldly concerns and focus more on my spiritual growth. But I still love my family deeply and want to support them. How can I let go without abandoning my responsibilities?"

Bhog nodded, understanding her dilemma. "Anika, your desire for detachment is a sign that your higher chakras — especially the **Anahata (heart)** and **Sahasrara (crown)** — are calling you to spiritual evolution. However, detachment does not mean abandoning love or responsibilities. In fact, the highest form of love, found in the Anahata chakra, is unconditional. It allows you to love without attachment, to care for your family without being weighed down by expectation or fear."

Anika listened carefully as Bhog continued. "The Sahasrara chakra, at the crown of the head, is where we experience unity with the divine, where we realize that everything is connected. In this state, you can care for your family and your spiritual growth simultaneously because you understand that both are part of the same whole. Detachment is not about leaving behind the world, but about rising above the ego's attachment to outcomes."

Anika smiled; her heart lightened by Bhog's wisdom. "Thank you, Bhog. I see now that detachment is not the same as disconnection."

Kalpana, the young child with wide eyes full of wonder, asked in her innocent voice, "Bhog, why do people feel scared sometimes? Does it come from the chakras too?"

The villagers chuckled softly at Kalpana's simple but profound question. Bhog's face lit up with a smile as he answered. "Yes, little one. Fear often comes from the Muladhara chakra, at the base of the spine. This chakra is connected to survival and safety. When we feel afraid, it is usually because we feel unsafe or insecure. It's the body's way of protecting us, but when we are too attached to fear, it can stop us from growing."

Kalpana blinked, absorbing the information. "Can I make the fear go away?"

Bhog smiled warmly. "Yes, Kalpana. You can calm fear by taking deep breaths and grounding yourself in the present moment. Fear is like a cloud — it comes and goes. When you feel it, just breathe, and remind yourself that you are safe."

Maya, the younger child, raised her hand eagerly. "Bhog, if fear is from the base, what about when we feel happy and light? Where does that come from?"

Bhog chuckled softly. "Ah, happiness comes from many places, Maya. When you feel light and joyful, it is often because your heart chakra, Anahata, is open. This chakra is where love and joy flow freely, allowing you to feel connected to others and the world around you. It is the source of kindness, compassion, and the sense of being at peace."

The conversation continued, weaving through questions from all ages. As the discussion deepened, Bhog brought it all together.

"My dear friends," Bhog said, his voice filled with warmth and wisdom, "we are all on a journey from Muladhara, the root, to Sahasrara, the crown. Along the way, we must balance the energies of Ida and Pingala and keep our chakras open and aligned. Fear and desire are part of this journey, but as we grow, we learn to transcend them, moving from survival to love, from love to wisdom, and from wisdom to unity with the divine."

The villagers sat in silence for a moment, reflecting on Bhog's words. They had learned that the chakras and energies within them were not just abstract ideas, but living, breathing aspects of their own lives. The children, the teenagers, the middle-aged, and the elders had all found answers to their deepest questions, and they now carried the tools to balance the energies within them as they continued their journeys.

As the day continued, the banyan tree stood tall, a symbol of stability, wisdom, and growth for all those who had gathered beneath its branches.

Fear and Desire

After a moment of silence, Amara, who had been reflecting on her struggles with ambition and introspection, spoke up. " Bhog, we just talked about the chakras and the energy channels. But I've been thinking more about the forces of fear and desire. How do they influence us on our spiritual journey? Can they be mapped to Ida and Pingala as well?"

Bhog, with a knowing smile, nodded. "Ah, yes, Amara, fear and desire are powerful forces in our lives. They shape many of our thoughts and actions. These two forces are deeply connected to Ida and Pingala — the two primary energy channels in our body. Fear aligns with Ida, which is connected to introspection, the mind, and the cooling, passive energy of the moon. Desire, on the other hand, is linked to Pingala, the active, fiery energy associated with the sun. Together, they create the duality that shapes much of human experience."

Ravi, always eager to understand more, leaned forward. "Bhog, how exactly does fear arise from Ida? I thought Ida was supposed to bring calmness and peace?"

Bhog smiled gently at Ravi's question. "It's true, Ravi, that Ida governs the mind and introspection. But when Ida becomes overactive or imbalanced, it can lead to excessive thinking, overanalyzing, and emotional withdrawal. This creates a contraction of energy, causing fear. Fear is a natural response when we become too focused on preserving what we have, withdrawing into the safety of our thoughts, and avoiding risk. When fear dominates, our energy becomes trapped in the lower chakras, particularly the Muladhara chakra, which is concerned with survival."

Kartik, thinking of his own struggles with ambition, asked, "And what about desire, Bhog? How does Pingala fit into this? I often feel driven by desire, whether it's for success or for providing for my family."

Bhog turned his gaze to Kartik. "Desire is the expansive force that drives action. Pingala, associated with the sun and the sympathetic nervous system, governs our ambition and desire for fulfillment. When Pingala is active, it pushes energy upward, motivating us to seek, achieve, and evolve. It's the force that propels us beyond basic survival toward higher states of being. But when desire is unbalanced, it can lead to overexertion, stress, and the constant pursuit of material goals without inner peace."

Anika, the elder, raised her hand. "Bhog, as we get older, fear and desire seem to evolve. When we are young, fear is about survival, and desire is about achieving goals. But as I grow older, I find myself reflecting more on my past. How does the journey through the chakras help us transcend these forces?"

Bhog smiled warmly at Anika's wisdom. "Indeed, Anika, fear and desire change as we move through life. The journey from Muladhara to Sahasrara, from the base chakra to the crown, can be seen as a path of balancing and eventually transcending fear and desire. At Muladhara, fear is predominant, as it is focused on self-preservation. As we move up to Svadhishthana, desire emerges — associated with pleasure and the exploration of our physical existence."

He paused for a moment, letting the words sink in before continuing. "In Manipura, desire becomes ambition and the need to assert ourselves in the world. But as we reach Anahata, the heart chakra, we begin to balance these forces with love and compassion, transcending the self-centered drives of the lower chakras. By the time we reach Vishuddha, we express truth and creativity, harmonizing fear of judgment with the desire to be heard."

Yash, the teenager, chimed in with a more personal question. "Bhog, sometimes I feel fear and desire pulling me in different directions. I want to succeed and be liked, but I'm also afraid of failing or being judged. How can I find balance?"

Bhog's eyes softened as he addressed Yash. "What you're feeling, Yash, is the natural conflict between Ida and Pingala — the forces of fear and desire. As you move through life, both forces will challenge you. But the key to balance is to recognize that both are necessary. Fear helps us avoid danger, while desire pushes us toward growth. The challenge is not to let one dominate the other. Through practices like Nadi Shodhana, alternate nostril breathing, you can balance the energies of Ida and Pingala, reducing the extremes of fear and desire. This will help you act with confidence while staying grounded in wisdom."

Maya, the youngest among the group, raised her hand with an innocent curiosity. "Bhog, is it scary to go from fear to desire? What happens when you reach the top, the crown?"

The group chuckled softly at Maya's question, and Bhog responded with a twinkle in his eye. "Ah, Maya, it's not scary if you understand that fear and desire are just parts of the journey. As we move from the root chakra to the crown chakra, we learn to balance them. When we reach the Sahasrara, the crown chakra, something wonderful happens — fear and desire dissolve. We no longer see them as separate forces. The energies of Ida and Pingala merge into the central channel, Sushumna, allowing the Kundalini energy to rise. In this state, there is no fear or desire — only peace and oneness with everything."

Radha, who had been listening quietly, finally spoke. "Bhog, you've talked about the importance of balancing fear and desire. How can we bring this understanding into our daily lives? It's easy to feel balanced while listening to you, but harder when we return to the chaos of life."

Bhog looked at Radha with understanding. "The practice begins here, Radha, but it continues in every moment of your life. Daily meditation and pranayama help balance the energies of Ida and Pingala. When fear arises, recognize it as a contraction of energy and breathe deeply to calm Ida. When desire overwhelms you, pause and bring awareness to your heart, balancing the drive of Pingala with the compassion of Anahata. Over time, this practice becomes a way of life. You will find yourself acting from a place of peace rather than reaction to fear or desire."

The villagers sat in quiet reflection, absorbing Bhog's teachings. He continued, guiding them through a simple meditation to balance these energies.

Bhog's Meditation for Balancing Fear and Desire

1. **Preparation and Grounding (Muladhara)**

   Bhog instructed the villagers to sit in a comfortable position, focusing on their breath. "Ground yourselves in the present moment. Feel the earth beneath you, supporting you. Let go of fear and restless craving and allow yourself to feel stable and safe."

2. **Observation of Thoughts (Svadhishthana)**

   "As you breathe, observe your thoughts. Notice any thoughts related to fear or desire. Simply watch them without judgment. Let them pass like clouds in the sky."

3. **Detachment from Thoughts (Manipura)**

   Bhog encouraged the villagers to gently detach from their thoughts. "When fear or desire arises, bring your awareness back to your breath. Let go of attachment to these thoughts and return to the present moment."

4. **Cultivating Compassion (Anahata)**

   "Now, bring your awareness to the heart center. Cultivate feelings of love and compassion for yourself and others. Feel the balance between fear and desire as they transform into understanding and kindness."

5. **Clarity and Truth (Vishuddha)**

   "Shift your focus to the throat chakra. Allow your breath to flow freely. If there are any truths you need to express to yourself, let them emerge with clarity and kindness."

6. **Insight and Vision (Ajna)**

   Bhog guided the group to the third eye. "Now, focus on the space between your eyebrows. See beyond fear and desire. Realize that these are temporary states of the mind, and that your true nature lies beyond them."

7. **Surrender and Union (Sahasrara)**

   "Finally, let go completely. Surrender all efforts to the divine. In this state, fear and desire dissolve, and you are one with the universe. Feel the energy of Ida and Pingala

> merge into the central channel, Sushumna. Rest in the peace of unity."

As Bhog finished guiding the meditation, the villagers opened their eyes, feeling a deep sense of calm and balance. They had learned to embrace fear and desire, understanding that these forces, when balanced, lead to spiritual growth and transformation.

The sun was now higher in the sky, casting a golden glow over the village. The day's teachings had left everyone with a renewed sense of purpose, and they rose slowly, ready to carry Bhog's wisdom into their daily lives, balancing the energies of Ida and Pingala with every breath they took.

Bhog adds, his voice calm yet filled with gravitas. "My dear friends, we have explored the forces of fear and desire and how they are mapped onto the energies of Ida and Pingala. Let us take a step further and look at these same forces from another great teacher — Buddha. Like us, Buddha sought liberation from suffering, and his teachings provide a path to understanding and ultimately overcoming the forces of fear and desire."

Ravi, the eager teenager, had been the first to speak, his mind still spinning with questions from the previous day. "Bhog," he had asked, "yesterday we learned about desire through Ida and Pingala, but I've heard that Buddha sees desire differently. Why does he call it the root of suffering, when it also seems to push us forward?"

Bhog had smiled warmly at Ravi's question, appreciating the young man's desire to understand. "Yes, Ravi," he had replied. "In Buddha's teachings, desire — known as *tanha* — is seen as the root cause of suffering. While in yoga, we balance desire as a necessary energy, Buddha taught that desire creates attachment. And it is attachment that binds us to the cycle of suffering, or *samsara*. Desire — whether for sensual pleasures, material things, or even life itself — leads to dissatisfaction. Even when one desire is fulfilled, another takes its place, keeping us trapped in an endless cycle."

Ravi nodded thoughtfully, absorbing the idea, while Bhog continued to explain.

Amara, who had been reflecting on her own attachments in life, leaned forward next. "Bhog," she had said, "I feel like Buddha's teaching on desire resonates with me. I've often found that my attachment to success or relationships brings me more anxiety than joy. How can we begin to let go of these attachments without becoming detached from life itself?"

Bhog had looked at Amara with understanding. "Amara, you're touching on a key insight," he had said. "Buddha did not teach us to abandon life or stop caring about what we love. Instead, he showed us how to engage with life without clinging to outcomes. You can begin letting go by practicing *mindfulness*, being fully present in the moment without attaching yourself to future or past events. This is *Right Mindfulness*, one of the steps of Buddha's Eightfold Path. In this way, you can care deeply but not be bound by fear or desire."

As Amara had considered this, Yash, the young teenager, had raised his hand, his voice reflecting the struggles of adolescence. "Bhog, you've talked a lot about desire, but what about fear? Fear holds me back — whether it's fear of failure or fear of what others think. How does Buddha talk about fear, and how can I overcome it?"

Bhog had smiled softly at Yash's vulnerability. "Fear, Yash, arises from attachment, just like desire," he had explained. "In Buddha's teachings, fear is linked to the impermanence of life. We fear losing what we love or failing to achieve what we desire. But all fear stems from clinging to things that are temporary, whether it's reputation, relationships, or even our identity. By realizing that everything is in constant change, we reduce fear. Buddha taught that fear is an illusion created by attachment to impermanence."

Kartik, the middle-aged father who carried the weight of many responsibilities, had then spoken up. "Bhog," he had said, "I often feel like desire for success and fear of failure drive me at the same time. How do we balance the need to work hard for our families while following Buddha's teaching of letting go?"

Bhog had turned his gaze to Kartik with empathy. "Kartik, you're not alone in this tension between desire and fear," he had responded. "Buddha does not ask us to stop providing for our families or to abandon our responsibilities. What he teaches is to let go of attachment to the outcome. It's about doing your *dharma* — your duty — without being attached to the results. This is *Right Intention* and *Right Action* in the Eightfold Path. When you act from a place of clear intention, without attachment, you free yourself from the suffering of both fear and desire."

Anika, the elder, had been quiet until now, listening deeply. When she spoke, her voice carried the weight of experience. "Bhog," she had said, "Buddha speaks of impermanence, and I feel it more as I grow older. I see the changes in my body, in the world, and even in my loved ones. How can we come to peace with this impermanence, especially when it feels painful?"

Bhog had softened his tone as he addressed Anika. "Anika," he had said, "what you are feeling is the core of Buddha's teaching. The pain of impermanence comes from our attachment to things staying the same. Buddha taught that *anicca* — the truth of impermanence — is something we must accept. But acceptance does not mean we stop loving or caring. It means we understand that all things change, and we let go of our need to control them.

Through *Right Understanding* and meditation, we find peace in the present moment, knowing that change is the only constant."

Kalpana, the youngest among them, had raised her hand with an innocent question. "Bhog," she had asked, "if everything changes, does that mean love changes too? What about the love we have for our family?"

The villagers had smiled at her innocence, and Bhog had answered with warmth. "Ah, Kalpana," he had said, "love changes too, but that doesn't make it any less real. Buddha taught that when we love without attachment, it becomes unconditional. When we cling to someone, fearing their change or loss, that is not true love — it is attachment. True love, the kind that comes from the heart, is free, open, and compassionate. It changes and grows, just like everything else."

Radha, who had always cared deeply for her family, had spoken next. "Bhog," she had said, "I've always found joy in caring for my family, but sometimes I worry too much. How do we care deeply without becoming consumed by fear or desire?"

Bhog had looked at Radha with compassion. "Radha," he had said, "your love for your family is a beautiful thing, but attachment can lead to worry and suffering. The key is to love without clinging. Buddha taught us to practice compassion — *karuna* — which is love without attachment. You can care deeply for others without fearing loss or trying to control outcomes. By practicing mindfulness and compassion, you can be present with your family without being consumed by worry."

Finally, Maya, the youngest child, had asked with wide-eyed curiosity, "Bhog, when all the fear and desire go away, what's left? Is it like when the sun comes out and makes everything bright?"

Bhog had chuckled softly at her innocent metaphor. "Yes, Maya," he had said. "When fear and desire dissolve, what's left is peace — a bright and clear mind, like the sun shining after a storm. Buddha called this state *nirvana* — the extinguishing of all flames of suffering. In this state, there is no clinging, no fear, only peace and stillness."

With those final words, Bhog had looked around at the villagers, sensing that they had absorbed the depth of Buddha's teachings. "Remember, my friends," he had concluded, "whether through the path of yoga or the path of Buddha, the goal is the same: liberation from suffering. Buddha's teachings show us that by letting go of attachment, we can find peace. Through mindfulness, compassion, and the acceptance of impermanence, we can live fully in the present moment, free from the chains of fear and desire."

The villagers had sat in silence, reflecting on Bhog's words. The morning light had filtered through the banyan tree, casting a gentle glow on the village. Slowly, they had risen, carrying with them a sense of peace and understanding. As they left, they knew they were not just hearing teachings but learning to live them, step by step, on their own journey toward freedom from fear and desire.

Three bodies, five sheaths

Next Day, The sun had barely risen, casting a soft glow over the village. Under the ancient banyan tree, Bhog once again sat with his seekers, ready to guide them through another day of spiritual exploration. The villagers — young and old — gathered in anticipation, their minds still filled with the teachings from the day before. Today, Bhog was to explain the complexities of the three bodies, the koshas, and the interplay of gunas and doshas.

Ravi couldn't hold back his curiosity. "Bhog," he began, "yesterday you explained the forces of fear and desire, but I've been wondering about the different layers of our being. I've heard about the Gross Body and the Subtle Body, but I don't understand how they all work together. Can you help us make sense of it?"

Bhog smiled and began to tell a story. "Once, there was a wise man named Arjuna who lived in a small village much like this one. Arjuna was respected for his wisdom, but he was troubled by an inner turmoil. His body ached, his mind was restless, and his heart was heavy with emotions. He visited a sage to seek answers.

The sage said, 'Arjuna, you are carrying the weight of many bodies. Your Gross Body is tired from the physical work of life. Your Subtle Body is burdened by your thoughts and emotions. And deep within, your Causal Body holds the seeds of karma that keep you tied to this suffering.'

'What can I do?' Arjuna asked, feeling overwhelmed.

The sage replied, 'You must learn to balance the gunas within you — sattva, rajas, and tamas — and free yourself from the layers that bind you.'

Arjuna followed the sage's advice. He practiced yoga to strengthen his physical body, pranayama to balance his energy, and meditation to calm his mind. Slowly, he began to feel lighter, not just in his body, but in his heart and soul. Over time, Arjuna realized that the layers of his being were like clouds — shifting and impermanent — and at the core of it all was a deep, unshakable peace."

The villagers listened quietly as Bhog finished the story, feeling the truth of Arjuna's journey reflected in their own lives.

Finally, Bhog brought the discussion back to the present.

Bhog, as usual, began by simplifying the concept for his listeners. "My dear friends," he said, his voice calm and steady, "today we will explore something that runs deep within us — the three bodies and the five koshas, or sheaths, that protect and surround our true self, the Atman. These koshas are layers that form an intricate web around the soul, much like how we dress in multiple layers of clothing during a cold winter. Each kosha serves its purpose, and each body provides a different aspect of our existence."

Ravi, the curious teenager who was always eager to ask questions, raised his hand. "Bhog, I've heard you speak of the Gross Body, the Subtle Body, and the Causal Body before. Can you explain how they connect with the koshas? Are they the same thing?"

Bhog smiled warmly. "Ah, Ravi, excellent question. The Gross Body, the Subtle Body, and the Causal Body are like three levels of our being, and these levels correspond to the five koshas. The koshas are the layers of protection or sheaths that cover these bodies and allow the Atman, or soul, to function in this world."

Bhog paused to tell a small story, drawing in the attention of the villagers.

"There was once a young man named Arya," Bhog began with a glint in his eye, "who had a dream one night. In his dream, he found himself dressed in many layers of clothing — five layers, to be exact. As he wandered through the dream, each layer began to take on a different role. One layer kept him warm and strong; another made him feel light and full of energy, and yet another seemed to make him feel joy and happiness. But as the dream continued, Arya realized that underneath all those layers, something more profound and true existed — the real him. And in his dream, he understood that these layers were necessary, but they were not the essence of who he truly was."

The villagers smiled at the story, understanding that Bhog was using the dream to explain the koshas in a simple way.

Bhog continued, turning back to the explanation. "The first of these layers is the **Annamaya Kosha**, which is the sheath of food. This is the layer that corresponds to the Gross Body, or Sthūla śharīra. It is made up of the five elements — earth, water, fire, air, and ether — and is nourished by the food we eat. This is the body that breathes, moves, and interacts with the physical world."

Kartik, the middle-aged father, nodded thoughtfully and asked, "Bhog, this Gross Body ages, weakens, and eventually dies, doesn't it? But what happens after that? What continues?"

Bhog responded, "Yes, Kartik, the Gross Body does indeed age and eventually die, but there is more to us than this physical body. Beyond the Gross Body is the Sūkṣma śharīra, the Subtle Body, which consists of three sheaths — the **Pranamaya Kosha** (the sheath of vital breath or energy), the **Manomaya Kosha** (the sheath of the mind), and the **Vijnanamaya Kosha** (the sheath of intellect and discernment). These sheaths continue even after the Gross Body is no longer with us."

Radha, always concerned for the well-being of her family, leaned forward. "Bhog, can you explain how the Subtle Body works with these sheaths? How do they influence our lives?"

Bhog nodded and continued. "The **Pranamaya Kosha** is the sheath of prana, the life force that energizes the Gross Body. It is through this kosha that we breathe, digest food, and circulate blood. It is the energy that animates us. Then comes the **Manomaya Kosha**, the sheath of the mind. This is where your thoughts, emotions, and desires live. It is the seat of your feelings, worries, and joys."

Amara, who often wrestled with emotional stress, asked, "Bhog, sometimes my mind feels so chaotic. Is that because of the **Manomaya Kosha**?"

Bhog smiled. "Yes, Amara. When your mind is restless, it is a sign that the Manomaya Kosha is out of balance. That's why practices like meditation and yoga are so important — they help calm the mind and restore balance to this sheath. And finally, we have the **Vijnanamaya Kosha**, which is the sheath of intellect and wisdom. This is where your discernment and understanding come from. It is the part of you that knows right from wrong and helps you make decisions."

Amara, feeling the weight of her own unbalanced mind, recalled a time when she had been overwhelmed with decisions. Her job, family, and responsibilities all seemed to clash, leaving her emotionally drained and mentally exhausted. After listening to Bhog's teachings on the koshas, she realized that her **Manomaya Kosha** — the sheath of the mind — had been in turmoil for some time.

Determined to bring balance back, Amara began a daily practice of pranayama and meditation. Slowly, she felt the shift. Her thoughts became clearer, her emotions more balanced, and for the first time in months, she felt in control of her mind. The calming of her **Manomaya Kosha** brought peace to her Subtle Body, and she felt a sense of alignment she hadn't experienced in a long time.

Bhog turned his attention to the third body, the **Karana śharīra**, or Causal Body. "The Causal Body," Bhog explained, "is the deepest and most subtle of the three bodies. It corresponds to the **Anandamaya Kosha**, the sheath of bliss. This is the body that holds the impressions from past experiences, and it is the seed from which the Subtle and Gross Bodies arise. It is also the body that connects you to universal consciousness. In this state, we experience bliss beyond individuality. It is said that in deep sleep, when the mind is still, we experience the peace of the **Anandamaya Kosha**."

Anika, the elder, asked, "Bhog, this bliss — can it only be experienced in deep sleep? Or can we feel it during our waking state as well?"

Bhog responded gently, "Anika, the bliss of the **Anandamaya Kosha** can be experienced not only in deep sleep but also in meditation and moments of deep spiritual connection. When your mind is still and your intellect is calm, you can touch this bliss even while awake. It is a state beyond thoughts, beyond emotions — a connection with the divine."

Anika had always been a seeker of peace, but in her old age, the worries of her children, grandchildren, and the village often clouded her mind. After listening to Bhog's explanation of the **Anandamaya Kosha**, she decided to try a deep meditation one afternoon.

As she sat in the stillness of her small home, she let go of her thoughts one by one, focusing only on her breath. Slowly, the thoughts that had once filled her mind disappeared, leaving behind a profound sense of peace. It wasn't sleep, and it wasn't waking — it was something beyond both. For the first time in her life, Anika touched the bliss of the **Anandamaya Kosha,** a deep, abiding joy that transcended her worries and fears.

Bhog finished his teaching for the day by bringing everything together. "So you see, my friends, we are much more than just this physical body. We are layers upon layers, each one serving its purpose in protecting the Atman, the true self. The Gross Body allows us to interact with the world, the Subtle Body helps us think, feel, and act, and the Causal Body connects us to the infinite bliss of the universe. By understanding these koshas and bodies, we can navigate life with more wisdom and peace."

As the villagers sat in reflection, they felt a deeper understanding of their existence. They now saw themselves not just as individuals moving through the world, but as complex beings, made up of many layers, each one playing a vital role in their journey through life.

"Now that we've understood the three bodies and five sheaths, we must also understand the influence of the gunas — **sattva, rajas, and tamas** — on these layers. These mental attributes shape how we interact with the world. **Sattva** brings clarity, peace, and balance; **rajas** brings energy and activity, but can also cause restlessness; and **tamas** brings inertia and ignorance."

Meera, who often struggled with energy imbalances, asked, "Bhog, how can we move from tamas to rajas and then to sattva? I feel like I'm always pulled between these energies."

Bhog answered with calm wisdom. "Meera, the key is in awareness. By practicing yoga, meditation, and mindfulness, you can move from the heavy inertia of **tamas** to the dynamic energy of **rajas**, and then finally to the calm, balanced state of **sattva**. This is the journey of balancing the koshas, gunas, and bodies. With time and dedication, you can transcend these layers and experience the deep peace that lies at the core of your being."

Bhog added "According to yoga, Stress is caused by the speed (**Vega**) of repetitive thoughts/ideas, which cause mental imbalances, resulting in agitation or negative emotional states. This mental unrest (**Manomaya Kosha**) would cause an imbalance in all other levels of existence. At the physical and energy levels (**Annamaya Kosa** and **Pranamaya Kosa**), excessive speed and demanding situations cause stress; at the emotional level (**Manomaya Kosa**), imbalances are caused by strong likes and dislikes; and at the psychological level (**Vijnanamaya Kosa**), conflicts and egocentric behavior are responsible for gross imbalances."

Yogic texts divide an individual's mental attributes (**Manomaya Kosha**) into three categories: sattva (flexibility), rajas (excitement), and Tamas (inertia/rigidity). According to scientific literature, various psychiatric disorders are characterized by the dominance of different gunas.

As the day continued under the banyan tree, the villagers sat in quiet reflection. They had learned about their bodies, minds, and spirits — woven together in a tapestry of existence. Bhog's teachings resonated deeply with them, as they began to see their lives not as a single story, but as a rich interplay of layers, waiting to be understood and balanced. Slowly, they rose, carrying the wisdom of the day into their hearts, ready to embark on the journey of restoring harmony across the layers of their existence.

Amid increasing awareness while the discourse a question arose from people "What are gunas and doshas, how are they correlated? How do they affect our health and what all can we do to keep them in balance?"

Bhog responded "Yogic texts also prescribe a detailed lifestyle management plan to restore balance at the guna level. It is believed that the mind should progress from **tamas** to **rajas**, then to **sattva**, and finally to **gunatita** (transcending gunas). In another study involving people with anxiety disorders, the clinical sample had high rajasic and tamasic factors, which were associated with a lower quality of life. Previous research has also found a link between VPI scores, psychological constructs, and mental health conditions, indicating that the five-factor model of personality traits is similar to guna-based assessments."

Doshas and Gunas

Bhog began with a soft tone, ensuring everyone was at ease. "Dear friends," he said, "let's talk about something that directly impacts our physical and mental well-being — **doshas and gunas**. These are the subtle energies that shape our constitution and influence our thoughts, emotions, and health. Understanding these energies is the key to living in balance."

Amara, as usual, was the first to ask a question. "Bhog, I've heard of Vata, Pitta, and Kapha, but I don't fully understand how they relate to the body and mind. Could you explain how these doshas affect us?"

Bhog smiled and nodded. "Ah, Amara, that's a good place to start. The doshas — Vata, Pitta, and Kapha — are the three energies that govern our physical constitution. Each of us has a unique combination of these doshas, which determines our natural state of balance, known as prakriti. When these doshas are balanced, we feel healthy, energetic, and peaceful. But when they are out of balance, we experience illness, stress, or emotional unrest."

Amara had always been an energetic and driven person, but lately, she had been feeling off-balance. Her sleep was restless, and she often felt irritable and overheated. After hearing Bhog's teachings on doshas, she began to wonder if her Pitta dosha — associated with fire and heat — was out of balance.

Amara approached Bhog after the gathering and asked for his guidance. He suggested she adopt cooling practices — gentle yoga poses, calming pranayama, and a cooling diet with foods like cucumber, mint, and coconut. Within weeks, Amara noticed a profound change. Her irritability subsided, her sleep improved, and she felt more in control of her emotions. The balance of her Pitta dosha had been restored.

Bhog continued, addressing the group. "Now, let's go deeper into what each dosha represents. Vata is linked to air and space, governing movement and communication. When balanced, Vata brings creativity and flexibility. But when it is out of balance, you may experience anxiety, dryness, or joint pain."

Ravi, always full of energy and curiosity, chimed in. "Bhog, sometimes I feel restless and can't seem to focus. Could that be my Vata dosha?"

Bhog smiled at Ravi's eagerness. "Yes, Ravi. Restlessness and difficulty focusing are signs that your Vata may be imbalanced. For someone like you, it's important to engage in grounding practices — gentle yoga, pranayama, and eating warm, nourishing foods to bring balance."

Ravi had always been an active young man, moving from one thing to the next with an almost endless supply of energy. But as he grew older, he began to feel more anxious and scattered. His thoughts raced, and he struggled to focus on his studies.

After hearing Bhog explain the concept of **Vata dosha**, Ravi realized that his fast-paced lifestyle was aggravating his Vata energy. He began practicing grounding yoga poses, like seated forward bends and restorative postures, and made an effort to eat warm, oily foods. Over time, Ravi felt calmer, more centered, and able to focus with clarity. His restlessness had transformed into a steady flow of creativity and focus.

Bhog then shifted the conversation to **Pitta dosha**, which is associated with fire and water. "Pitta governs digestion, metabolism, and transformation. When in balance, it brings clarity, courage, and determination. But when it is out of balance, it can cause anger, irritability, or inflammation."

Kartik, the middle-aged father who often struggled with anger, raised his hand. "Bhog, I sometimes feel overwhelmed with anger, especially when things don't go as planned. Is my Pitta dosha too high?"

Bhog nodded. "Yes, Kartik. Excessive anger and frustration are signs of an aggravated **Pitta**. To cool this fire, you need to focus on calming practices — gentle yoga, cooling pranayama techniques like Sheetali and Sheetkari, and a diet that avoids hot, spicy foods."

Kartik, as a father and a provider, often found himself in stressful situations that would ignite his temper. After learning about the Pitta dosha and how it relates to fire, he realized that his anger was a sign of imbalance.

Following Bhog's advice, Kartik started incorporating cooling practices into his daily routine. He replaced spicy foods with cooling ones, practiced calming breathwork, and engaged in relaxing evening walks. Slowly, he noticed his anger subsiding, and in its place, a sense of calm determination emerged. His Pitta was back in balance, and so was his approach to life.

Bhog then moved on to explain **Kapha**, the dosha associated with water and earth. "Kapha provides structure and stability. It is the energy of grounding, lubrication, and strength. When in balance, Kapha brings calmness, patience, and endurance. But when it is out of balance, it can lead to lethargy, weight gain, and resistance to change."

Anika, the wise elder of the village, spoke next. "Bhog, sometimes I feel heavy and slow, like I don't have the energy I once did. Is that my Kapha dosha acting up?"

Bhog responded with kindness. "Yes, Anika. When Kapha is imbalanced, it can make you feel sluggish and unmotivated. The key is to introduce more movement and lightness into your life —

practice energizing yoga poses like sun salutations, use stimulating pranayama like **Bhastrika**, and eat lighter, spicier foods to boost your energy."

Anika had always been the steady, grounding presence in the village, but as she aged, she noticed a heaviness creeping into her life. She felt slow, tired, and resistant to change. After hearing Bhog's teachings on Kapha dosha, she realized that her Kapha had become imbalanced.

She began practicing invigorating yoga sequences and incorporated more stimulating foods into her diet. She also embraced changes in her daily routine, introducing more variety and excitement. In time, Anika's energy returned, and she felt light and vibrant once again.

Bhog then brought the conversation full circle, explaining the connection between the doshas and the gunas. "Just as the doshas govern the body, the gunas — sattva, rajas, and tamas — govern the mind. Sattva represents clarity and purity, rajas represent activity and restlessness, and tamas represents inertia and darkness. Our goal is to balance both the doshas and the gunas, so we can live in harmony with ourselves and the world around us."

Meera, a young mother who often felt overwhelmed by her responsibilities, asked, "Bhog, how do we balance these energies? I feel pulled in so many directions — how do I know what practices are right for me?"

Bhog answered with wisdom. "Meera, it all begins with awareness. Pay attention to your body and mind. If you feel restless, focus on grounding practices. If you feel lethargic, bring in more energy. Use yoga, pranayama, meditation, and lifestyle adjustments to bring balance. When you know your prakriti — your unique constitution — you can tailor your practices to suit your needs."

Meera, a mother of two young children, often found herself torn between her family, work, and personal life. She felt like she was constantly running on empty, with no time to focus on herself. After learning about the doshas and gunas from Bhog, Meera began to make small changes in her routine.

She practiced calming yoga in the mornings to start her day with balance, ate nourishing foods, and incorporated moments of mindfulness throughout her day. Slowly, she found that she had more energy and clarity, and her mind was no longer overwhelmed by the demands of life. She had found her balance.

As Bhog concluded the day's teachings, he left the villagers with a final thought. "Understanding your doshas and gunas is not just about healing the body and mind — it is about connecting with your true nature. When you know who you are and what you need, you can live in harmony, both within yourself and with the world around you. Balance is the key, and the path is one of awareness, mindfulness, and self-compassion."

The villagers, filled with new insights, rose from their spots beneath the banyan tree, ready to bring balance to their lives through the wisdom of the doshas and gunas. They knew that with Bhog's guidance, they were not just learning — they were transforming.

Swara Yoga

Bhog's pursuit was not of material wealth but of the profound knowledge hidden within the ancient teachings of Swara Yoga. His simple dwelling, adorned with spiritual scriptures and symbols, became a haven for seekers who yearned to explore the depths of breath and consciousness.

As the tranquil village prepared for the transition from Shukla Paksha to Krishna Paksha, a time marked by the shifting dance of the moon and the sun, Bhog felt an inner calling to share the transformative wisdom of Swara Yoga with his fellow people.

Gathering beneath the sacred banyan tree, Bhog began to narrate a tale that intertwined the cosmic rhythms with the breath. He spoke of Ida, the left nostril, dancing in harmony with the waxing moon during Shukla Paksha, and of Pingala, the right nostril, embracing solar energy during Krishna Paksha.

As Bhog spoke, the people closed their eyes, immersing themselves in the imagery of the celestial ballet within. They felt the subtle transitions, the gentle dance from one nostril to the other, mirroring the cyclical rhythm of the moon and the sun.

In the midst of the crowd, a curious young farmer named Kavi found himself captivated by the notion of aligning breath with cosmic energies. Bhog, recognizing Kavi's eagerness, took him under his wing, guiding him through the practices of Swara Yoga. Together, they explored the connection between breath and the changing phases of the moon.

With each passing lunar cycle, Kavi noticed a profound shift within himself – a calmness that echoed the tranquility of the village. Inspired by Kavi's newfound serenity, the people eagerly embraced the teachings of Swara Yoga.

What is Swara Yoga?

Bhog started his discourse on "Swara Yoga"

"Today, we will explore the deep, ancient science of **Swara Yoga** — a profound journey into the very breath that sustains us, connects us to the universe, and reveals the hidden wisdom of the cosmos. This is not just a practice of breath control as we know in Pranayama; it is a complete system that delves into the mysteries of life, cosmic energy, and the rhythms of the universe itself.

Let us begin by understanding the essence of Swara Yoga. The word **"Swara"** is derived from Sanskrit, meaning sound or note. It is also the continuous flow of air through one nostril at a time. Now, **Yoga** means union — union of the body, mind, and spirit. So, **Swara Yoga** is the science that enables the realization of cosmic consciousness through the control and manipulation of breath. While **Pranayama** involves controlling the breath in various ways, Swara Yoga goes much deeper — it links the breath to the rhythms of the sun, moon, the changing seasons, and even our mental and physical conditions.

In Swara Yoga, we observe, study, and manipulate the breath or **Swara** to align ourselves with the greater forces of nature. The flow of breath through each nostril has profound implications on our energies, activities, and overall balance. This practice is comprehensive, connecting our breath to the **cosmic cycles** and individual **states of being**.

The Lunar and Solar Cycles: Shukla Paksha and Krishna Paksha

Swara Yoga teaches us that the flow of breath through the left nostril, called **Ida Nadi**, is associated with the **lunar energy**, and the right nostril, or **Pingala Nadi**, is connected to the **solar energy**. The moon and the sun, dear seekers, govern much more than just the tides or daylight — they influence our very being.

Let us first consider the **Shukla Paksha**, the waxing phase of the moon. During this phase, it is believed that the **left nostril**, or **Ida Nadi**, becomes dominant. The lunar energy flows freely, bringing calmness, receptivity, and a cooling effect on the mind and body. This is the time for introspection, for spiritual practices, for meditation, and for turning inward. The gentle pull of the moon makes this an ideal period for mental work and for focusing on **internal growth**.

On the other hand, during the **Krishna Paksha**, the waning phase of the moon, the **right nostril** or **Pingala Nadi** becomes more active. This is the solar energy at work — bringing vitality, physical strength, and a heating effect. During this time, we are more suited for outward activities — engagement with the world, physical work, productivity, and tasks that require energy and vigor.

The Science of Swara: Cycles, Transitions, and Timing

Swara Yoga is precise, and to practice it well, one must pay attention to the transitions of breath. Just as the moon and sun influence the waxing and waning of energies, there is a **natural daily cycle** where the breath alternates between the left and right nostrils every 1.5 to 2 hours. This rhythmic alternation corresponds to the body's natural rhythms and the cosmos' eternal dance.

The transitions during **sunrise** and **sunset** are particularly significant, when the breath briefly flows through the **Sushumna Nadi**, the central channel of the spine. It is during these moments, when neither Ida nor Pingala dominates, that one experiences the most **balance** — a momentary union of the lunar and solar energies within. These are auspicious times for deep meditation and spiritual practices, for it is here that one can touch the core of the **cosmic truth**.

Furthermore, on special days like **Amavasya** (new moon), the right nostril, or **Pingala**, dominates strongly, influencing both our internal energies and how we interact with the world. Swara Yoga teaches us that the breath is not random but a deeply ordered reflection of the larger universe.

Observing and Understanding the Swaras

To become proficient in Swara Yoga, one must first learn the art of **observation**. You must observe how the breath flows through the nostrils, note the **dominant nostril**, and learn to adjust your activities accordingly. For instance, when the **left nostril** dominates, it is a time for **introspection** — meditation, calm mental work, and spiritual practices will yield the best results. Conversely, when the **right nostril** is dominant, you are better suited for **physical tasks**, external engagements, and activities that require action and energy.

Regular observation of the Swaras helps you attune to your natural rhythm. You begin to see that the body, mind, and breath are not separate from the cosmic forces — they are, in fact, **expressions** of those very forces. Through this observation, you will gain **awareness** of the changing energies within and around you, and how best to channel them in harmony with the universe.

Balancing the Breath: The Practice of Nadi Shodhana

While the Swaras alternate naturally throughout the day, there are times when imbalance may occur — one Swara may dominate for too long, leading to physical or mental disturbances. In such cases, we turn to the practice of **Nadi Shodhana**, or alternate nostril breathing. This practice, dear seekers, is a powerful way to **balance** the lunar and solar energies within. It harmonizes **Ida** and **Pingala**, restoring equilibrium to the body and mind.

In **Nadi Shodhana**, we consciously regulate the flow of breath, alternating between the left and right nostrils. This helps to remove blockages from the **Nadis**, purify the energetic channels, and bring about a sense of **inner peace** and **balance**.

The Cosmic Harmony of Swara Yoga

Dear seekers, Swara Yoga is not just about breath; it is a way to connect with the **cosmic rhythm** that underlies all of creation. By aligning the flow of your breath with the cycles of the sun, moon, and seasons, you tap into a deeper layer of existence. You begin to **move with the universe**, not against it. You learn when to engage, when to withdraw, when to act, and when to meditate.

Swara Yoga teaches us that life is a dance of energies — the **lunar** and **solar**, the **internal** and **external**, the **calm** and the **active**. By mastering the Swaras, you do not merely control the breath; you master the art of living in harmony with the **cosmic forces**.

Creation, dear seekers, is not random. It is driven by subtle forces — the Tattwas — that shape everything we see and experience. The universe itself originates from a single, birthless, formless existence. From this supreme source, **Akasha** (ether) emerges. From Akasha arises **Vayu** (air), and from Vayu comes **Tejas** (fire). Tejas gives rise to **Apas** (water), and from Apas emerges **Prithvi** (earth). These five elements are the building blocks of creation, not just on a cosmic scale but also within our own being.

These **five Mahabhutas** — ether, air, fire, water, and earth — are spread throughout the universe, forming, sustaining, and eventually dissolving everything. Creation is a continuous, ceaseless process that begins with Tattwas, is sustained by them, and finally dissolves back into them. Every object, every being, is a dance of these elements in various proportions.

This is the cycle of life, seekers. Creation, sustenance, and dissolution — this is the cosmic rhythm, and it is mirrored in our bodies and in the flow of our breath.

Mahabhutas and Our Psychic Body

Now, let us turn inward. These five elements — Mahabhutas — not only exist in the external world but also shape our **psychic body**. Each of the Mahabhutas corresponds to a particular **Nadi** or energy channel in our body, and Swara Yoga links the flow of these Nadis to the **phases of the moon**, the **Sun**, and even the influence of **planets**.

In Swara Yoga, we understand that when a planet affects the earth's gravitational or electromagnetic fields, it also alters the energy patterns in our body. This change can be perceived as a shift in the flow of our breath. The **Swaras**, or the flow of breath through the nostrils, represent the influence of the elements within us. When the Swaras are aligned with the natural cycles, our energies are balanced. When they are disrupted, we experience physical and mental disturbances.

The **breath cycle** is a reflection of these cosmic influences. By observing and controlling the breath, we can balance the **subtle forces** within us. Swara Yoga offers us this tool — simple, yet deeply effective — to align with the cosmic dance of creation and dissolution.

The Influence of Tithis and Phases of the Moon

Now, let us consider the **Tithis**, the phases of the moon. The moon plays a vital role in Swara Yoga, as its phases affect the flow of breath through **Ida Nadi** (left nostril) and **Pingala Nadi** (right nostril). From **Amavasya** (new moon) to **Purnima** (full moon), we witness the **Shukla Paksha** — the bright phase of the moon. From **Purnima** back to **Amavasya**, we enter the **Krishna Paksha** — the dark phase.

During the **Shukla Paksha**, the **left nostril**, or Ida, tends to dominate, bringing cooling, calming lunar energy. In contrast, during the **Krishna Paksha**, the **right nostril**, or Pingala, becomes more active, channeling the heat and vitality of solar energy.

Each day of the lunar cycle, known as **Tithi**, has its own influence on the flow of the Swaras. The **first three days** of Shukla Paksha, for example, see the left nostril flowing at sunrise and the right at sunset. As we move through the cycle, this pattern alternates, linking the breath to the phases of the moon, and thus, the elemental forces within us.

The Role of Breath Control in Swara Yoga

Now, you may ask, "If all the Swaras change automatically with the time of day and the phases of the moon, what is the role of breath control? Why do we need to practice it?" A wise villager once posed this very question to me, and it is a question many of you may also have.

Let me explain while the **Swaras** naturally follow cosmic cycles, they are also deeply influenced by our **physical** and **mental states**. Depending on our health, our emotions, and our thoughts, the Swaras may drift from their ideal patterns. There will be times when only one nostril remains active for too long, or both nostrils may flow simultaneously indicating an imbalance, a disturbance at the **physical** or **mental level**.

In such cases, dear seekers, Swara Yoga provides us with a way to **correct** this imbalance. Think of it as a form of **reverse engineering**.

If we can bring the Swaras back into their ideal state — according to the time of day, the phase of the moon, or the activity we are engaged in — we can restore harmony to our body and mind.

For example, if you are feeling **anxious** and you notice that your **right nostril** (Pingala) is dominant, it means the **solar energy** is overpowering you, fueling the agitation. By consciously switching the breath to flow through the **left nostril** (Ida), you will invoke the **calming lunar energy**, and within moments, you will feel more at peace. Similarly, this principle applies to various physical and mental conditions.

The Cosmic Connection of Breath

In this way, dear seekers, **Swara Yoga** becomes not just a tool for physical and mental well-being but a way to **tune in to the cosmos**. By aligning our breath with the **Tattwas** and the **Mahabhutas**, we tap into the same forces that created the universe. Every breath you take is a reflection of the **cosmic process** — creation, sustenance, and dissolution, over and over again.

We are constantly in a dance with the universe, whether we realize it or not. Swara Yoga brings this dance into conscious awareness. When we **observe** the flow of our breath, we are not merely noticing an internal function — we are witnessing the **play of the elements**, the **cycles of the moon and sun**, and the **influence of the planets** upon our own being. We become aware of the **subtle forces** that govern not just the external world, but the very fabric of our inner world as well.

Harmonizing the Elements Within

Ultimately, dear seekers, Swara Yoga gives us the power to **harmonize** the five elements — ether, air, fire, water, and earth — within us. By balancing the breath and the **Swaras**, we balance the energies of **Ida** and **Pingala**, aligning ourselves with the rhythms of the universe. This harmony brings **health**, **clarity of mind**, and **spiritual alignment**.

So, remember this: **Tattwas** may form and dissolve the universe, but through the breath, we can influence the **Tattwas** within us. When you master the **flow of breath**, you master your connection to the cosmos.

Let your breath be your guide, let it align you with the eternal forces, and may it bring you into balance with the rhythm of creation. In every breath, you hold the power of the universe — its creation, its sustenance, and its dissolution."

Bhog continued, his voice as calm and steady as the morning itself. " This system teaches us that life is a dance of energies — the lunar and solar, the calm and the active, the internal and the external. Through the Swaras, or breath channels, we can harmonize ourselves with the forces of the cosmos. But Swara Yoga is not merely about breath control; it is about mastering the art of living in harmony with the universe."

Ravi, eager as always, was the first to raise a question. "Bhog, if our breath flows automatically through our nostrils in a particular pattern, why do we need to control it? Isn't everything happening naturally?"

Bhog smiled at Ravi's keen observation. "Ah, Ravi, you're right to ask this. You see, the Swaras — our breath through the right and left nostrils — do follow a natural cycle, influenced by the time of day, the lunar phases, and even planetary positions. However, when our physical or mental health is disturbed, this natural flow becomes imbalanced. At times, one nostril may dominate for too long, or both may become active simultaneously, which can signal a disorder. By consciously controlling the breath, we can bring balance back to our body and mind, much like tuning a musical instrument to restore harmony."

Ravi, always seeking to understand more deeply, decided to test Bhog's teachings for himself. One evening, he felt particularly anxious — his mind racing with worries about his future. He remembered Bhog's words and checked his breath. Sure enough, his right nostril, the solar channel, was active.

Ravi sat down, closed his eyes, and began consciously shifting his breath to his left nostril, the lunar channel. He practiced this for a few minutes, focusing on calm, deep breaths. As he did, something remarkable happened: his racing thoughts began to slow, and a sense of peace washed over him. The anxiety that had gripped him loosened its hold. Ravi realized in that moment the power of breath to transform not just the body, but the mind.

Amara, seated nearby, was listening closely. She had always struggled with balancing her emotions, especially during the lunar phases. "Bhog," she asked, "how do the phases of the moon affect the flow of our breath? And can this really impact how we feel?"

Bhog nodded. "Yes, Amara. The moon and its phases have a profound effect on our body and mind. In Swara Yoga, we recognize that the lunar and solar energies alternate throughout the day and night. Like I said before, during certain phases of the moon, the left nostril, which is associated with Ida Nadi and lunar energy, becomes more dominant. On other days, the right nostril, linked to Pingala Nadi and solar energy, takes over. The shifting phases of the moon — from the new moon to the full moon — guide this process. When we understand this cycle, we can work with it, rather than against it."

Amara, sensitive to the rhythms of nature, had long noticed that her mood would shift with the phases of the moon. On full moon nights, she often felt restless, unable to sleep, while on the dark nights of the new moon, she would become introspective, sometimes even melancholic.

After Bhog's explanation, she decided to experiment. On the next full moon, Amara spent the evening practicing left nostril breathing to activate the calming lunar energy. She also incorporated more calming activities — gentle yoga, quiet reflection — and found that her restlessness subsided. The following morning, she felt refreshed and balanced, in harmony with the natural rhythms she had once resisted.

Anika, the village elder who had always been curious about the connection between breath and health, asked, "Bhog, how can we use this knowledge to heal ourselves when we feel out of balance? For example, if I'm feeling sluggish, what should I do?"

Bhog turned his kind gaze toward Anika. "Ah, Anika, excellent question. When you feel sluggish, it's often because the Kapha dosha, related to earth and water, has become too dominant. In this case, you would activate the solar breath, or right nostril, to bring more fire and air into your system. This energizes and stimulates the body, breaking through the heaviness."

Anika had recently been feeling more tired than usual, struggling to find the energy for her daily chores. After hearing Bhog's advice, she decided to practice right nostril breathing in the mornings to activate her solar energy.

For several days, she sat quietly at sunrise, breathing deeply through her right nostril. As the days passed, Anika began to notice a shift. Her energy levels increased, and the fatigue that had weighed her down lifted. She felt lighter, more vibrant, and ready to face the day with renewed strength.

Radha, who often found herself feeling different emotions at various points in the month, asked, "Bhog, can we change how we feel by controlling the flow of breath in line with the lunar days?"

Bhog nodded. "Yes, Radha. For example, if during a Krishna Paksha day you feel heavy or dull, you can switch your breath to flow through the solar, or Pingala, channel to lift your energy. Likewise, during a Shukla Paksha day, if you feel overactive, you can switch to the lunar, or Ida, channel to calm yourself. This balance between lunar and solar is key to maintaining harmony in both body and mind."

Radha had always been aware of how her moods would shift with the moon's phases. During the waxing moon, she felt energized and productive, but as the moon waned, she often became sluggish and withdrawn.

After learning from Bhog, she decided to consciously change her breath according to the moon's cycle. On days when she felt too heavy, she practiced right nostril breathing to energize herself. And when she felt too restless, she focused on left nostril breathing to calm her mind. This practice helped her stay balanced, no matter where the moon was in its cycle.

As Bhog concluded his teaching, he left the villagers with one final thought. "Swara Yoga is more than just a technique of breath control. It is a way to live in harmony with the cosmic forces that shape our existence. By mastering the breath, we can master the dance of energies within us — the lunar and the solar, the active and the calm. And in doing so, we align ourselves with the rhythm of creation itself."

The villagers sat in quiet reflection, absorbing Bhog's words. They realized that their breath was not just a function of survival, but a powerful tool for self-healing and balance. With this knowledge, they were ready to bring harmony into their lives, one breath at a time.

Kalpana, one of the younger villagers, had been listening intently to Bhog's teachings on Swaras. She raised her hand and asked,

"Bhog, how can we manually change the Swaras? Is there a way to control which nostril is active?"

Bhog looked at Kalpana with a smile, appreciating her thoughtful question. "Yes, there are indeed ways to manually change the active Swara, or nostril, depending on which energy you want to activate — solar or lunar, Pingala or Ida. Let me explain a few simple methods that anyone can practice."

Kalpana had always been sensitive to changes in her body, especially how her breath would change depending on her mood. After listening to Bhog speak about the importance of breath control, she became curious. One evening, she noticed that during moments of stress, her breath was shallow and fast through her right nostril. This left her feeling agitated and restless. That's when she knew she had to ask Bhog about ways to change her breath and regain control.

Bhog explained, "The first method is called the Yoga Danda Method. This is a tool used to manually shift the breath flow from one nostril to the other."

He continued, "You take a yoga danda — an L-shaped wooden staff — and place it under the armpit of the active side. If, for example, your right nostril is active and you want to shift the flow to your left nostril, you place the danda under your right armpit and lean your weight on it. After a few minutes, you'll notice that your left nostril becomes active."

The villagers nodded, intrigued by the simplicity of the method. Anika, the elder, who had often observed her own breath patterns, asked, "Bhog, how long does it usually take for the change to happen?"

Bhog replied, "Ah, Anika, within 5 to 10 minutes, you'll notice a shift. It's a simple and effective way to control the flow of breath. If the shift doesn't happen, it could be an indication of some underlying imbalance in the energy channels."

Anika had always been a grounded presence in the village, but recently, she had been feeling out of sorts. After Bhog's lesson, she borrowed a yoga danda from a friend and decided to try it at home. One afternoon, she noticed that her right nostril was active, and she was feeling unusually agitated. She placed the danda under her right armpit and leaned her weight on it, as Bhog had taught. Within minutes, her breath shifted to the left nostril, and a sense of calm returned. It was as though a switch had been flipped, bringing her back to balance.

Bhog then moved on to the second method. "The next technique is the Lying Method. It's very simple. If you want to switch the active nostril, lie down on the side of the active nostril. For example, if your left nostril is active and you want to change to the right, lie down on your left side. Within 5 to 10 minutes, you'll notice that the right nostril becomes active."

Amara, who had often felt the need to calm herself before bedtime, asked, "Bhog, what happens if the breath doesn't change after 20 minutes?"

Bhog looked at her kindly. "Amara, if the breath doesn't change after 20 minutes, it could mean there's an imbalance in the energy flow. This imbalance can sometimes lead to physical or mental issues if not addressed. It's important to be aware of these signs and take steps to restore balance."

Amara often found it difficult to fall asleep, her mind racing with thoughts late into the night. After learning about the Lying Method, she decided to try it. One night, when her right nostril was active and she was feeling restless, she lay down on her right side, hoping to shift the breath to her left, calming Ida Nadi. Sure enough, after about 10 minutes, she felt the breath shift, and a wave of calm washed over her. That night, she slept peacefully, grateful for the newfound control over her breath.

Bhog continued with the third method, which caught the attention of the younger villagers. "The final technique is the Manual Pressure Method. You can manually apply pressure to the armpit of the active side using the opposite hand. For example, if your right nostril is active and you want to change to the left, press your right armpit with your left hand. Hold this pressure for a few minutes, and the breath will shift to the opposite nostril."

Yash, the energetic teenager who often found it difficult to calm his mind, asked eagerly, "Bhog, can I use this method anytime I feel anxious or stressed?"

Bhog smiled at Yash's enthusiasm. "Yes, Yash, this method works well in moments of stress or anxiety. If you find that your right nostril is active and you're feeling agitated, apply this technique, and it will help shift the breath to your left nostril, which promotes calm and balance."

Yash, like many teenagers, often felt overwhelmed by the pressures of school and life. One afternoon, he noticed that his right nostril was active and that his anxiety was building. He remembered Bhog's lesson and decided to try the Manual Pressure Method. Placing his left hand under his right armpit, Yash applied gentle pressure and waited. Slowly, his breath shifted, and as it did, the tension in his chest eased. Yash felt more relaxed, finally understanding the power of breath control.

Now Bhog began to tell them about how Swara Yoga can be applied in various aspects of life, using simple techniques and observations to maintain balance and attune to the natural order of the universe.

Everyday Applications of Swara Yoga

1. **Upon Waking Up**: When you first wake up, observe the flow of your breath. Which nostril is more active? If the **right nostril** is dominant, place your **right palm** against the right side of your face and gently touch it, keeping your eyes closed. If the **left nostril** is active, do the same with your **left palm**. This practice helps you attune to the energy you'll carry throughout the day. Then, depending on the active nostril, step out of bed with the corresponding foot — right foot if the right nostril flows, left foot if the left nostril flows.

2. **Using the Bathroom**: This might seem surprising, but even basic bodily functions like using the loo can benefit from Swara Yoga. When the **right nostril** (Pingala) is active, it is the ideal time for **bowel movements**, as Pingala is associated with activity and vitality. Similarly, when the **left nostril** (Ida) flows, it is best for urination, as the lunar energy of Ida brings calmness and fluidity.

3. **Eating and Drinking**: Swara Yoga provides specific guidelines for mealtime as well. When the **right nostril** flows, eat your meals. Pingala's solar energy supports digestion and physical processes. When the **left nostril** flows, drink water, as Ida supports hydration and cooling processes within the body.

4. **Going to Sleep and Waking Up**: Go to bed when the **right nostril** is active. This dominance of Pingala ensures restful sleep and supports the body's restorative processes during the night. When the **left nostril** is active, it is the ideal time to **wake up**, bringing calmness and a balanced state of mind to start the day.

5. **Leaving the House**: When stepping out of the house, always place the foot that corresponds to the active nostril first on the ground. If your **left nostril** flows, step out with your **left foot** first. If the **right nostril** is dominant, step with your **right foot**. This simple act aligns your energy with the external environment and ensures smoother outcomes.

6. **Journeys and Entering New Spaces**: For long journeys, begin when the **left nostril** flows, as the lunar energy of Ida supports endurance and safety. When entering a new house or starting something new, wait until the **right nostril** (Pingala) is dominant. The active solar energy will help ensure success in new ventures.

7. **Daily Rhythms**: During the **day**, the dominance of the **left nostril** is considered auspicious, as Ida fosters calm, introspective activities. At **night**, the dominance of the **right nostril** promotes good health and longevity.

8. **Public Speaking, Studying, and Learning**: When the **right nostril** is dominant, it is an excellent time for external activities like **public speaking**, **studying**, or **learning**. The Pingala energy enhances focus, communication, and retention of knowledge.

9. **Spiritual Practices and Auspicious Work**: Meditation, mantra chanting, and the beginning of any spiritual or auspicious activity — such as building a house, moving into a new home, or starting a new business — are best done when the **left nostril** is dominant. Avoid performing external or material work when both nostrils are active, as this indicates that the **Sushumna Nadi** is open, which is ideal for spiritual practices but not for worldly tasks.

Swara Yoga and the Rhythms of Time

"Swara Yoga also aligns with the **lunar cycle**. The phases of the moon, especially **Tithis** (the different phases of the lunar month), have a direct impact on the flow of breath. In the **Shukla Paksha** (the waxing moon), your **left nostril** is more active at sunrise, while during the **Krishna Paksha** (the waning moon), your **right nostril** takes dominance at sunrise.

Each **Tithi** — such as **Pratipada**, **Dwitiya**, **Ashtami**, and so on — corresponds with specific nostril dominance at different times of the day. For example, during the dark fortnight of **Krishna Paksha**, the right nostril flows more frequently. Similarly, during **Shukla Paksha**, the left nostril governs activities. By syncing your activities with these cycles, you conserve energy and maximize your efficiency.

Realigning Your Swara

Now, you may wonder — what if your Swara is not in harmony with these natural cycles? Swara Yoga provides tools for **realignment**. If you find that your breath is flowing through the wrong nostril, or both nostrils are active at the wrong time, you can make simple adjustments:

1. **Close the Active Nostril**: Use your finger or cotton wool to close the nostril that is flowing. This encourages the opposite nostril to activate.

2. **Pressure on the Armpit**: Apply light pressure to the armpit on the side of the active nostril to stimulate the opposite side.

3. **Posture**: Lie down on the side of the active nostril to redirect the flow of breath to the other nostril.

4. **Water Therapy**: A hot or cold bath can also help reset the flow of Swara.

5. **Food Choices**: Consuming specific foods can activate or calm your Swaras. For example, **chili** and **ginger** stimulate the **right nostril** (Pingala), while **yogurt** and **bananas** stimulate the **left nostril** (Ida).

Swara Yoga and Physical/Mental Health

Swara Yoga offers insight into the **physical** and **mental states** of the body. For example, if your **left nostril** is dominating for too long, you may experience cold-like symptoms. By consciously switching to the **right nostril**, you can counteract this imbalance. On the other hand, an overactive **right nostril** can lead to symptoms of **acidity** or **fever**. The breath, when properly controlled, can bring your body back into balance."

The aged seeker, his voice steady but filled with curiosity, spoke up. "Bhog, is there any connection between astrology and our breathing — the flow of Ida, Pingala, and Sushumna?"

Bhog smiled warmly at the question, pleased by the depth of the inquiry. "Ah, yes, dear ones," he began. "There is indeed a connection. In ancient spiritual traditions like yoga and tantra, it is believed that the flow of energy through the nadis — Ida, Pingala, and Sushumna — is influenced by the positions and movements of celestial bodies. The stars and planets, in their cosmic dance, create energies that affect not only our consciousness but also our physiology, especially through the breath."

The aged seeker, who had lived through many cycles of the moon and sun, had always been fascinated by astrology. As a child, he had learned from his father how the positions of the planets affected life on Earth. Over the years, he observed the subtle shifts in his energy as the moon waxed and waned. But something was still unclear to him — how these celestial movements influenced his breath. When Bhog began teaching Swara Yoga, the elder knew this was his chance to bridge the gap between his love for astrology and the mysteries of the breath.

Bhog continued, now addressing the entire village. “The flow of Ida and Pingala is deeply connected to the solar and lunar energies. Ida, as you know, is associated with the Moon, representing cooling, feminine, and receptive qualities. Pingala, on the other hand, is connected to the Sun, symbolizing heat, activity, and masculine energy. The flow of prana through these channels is influenced by planetary movements, particularly those of the Sun and Moon.”

Amara, who had always been curious about how astrology influenced her emotional states, asked, “Bhog, does that mean our breath changes with the phases of the Moon and Sun? Can this explain why we sometimes feel so different during these times?”

Bhog nodded, appreciating the insight in Kalpana’s question. “Yes, Amara. During the New Moon and Full Moon phases, the flow of energy through Ida and Pingala shifts. During the New Moon, lunar energy may dominate, influencing the flow of Ida and bringing a more introspective, cooling energy. Conversely, during the Full Moon, when the Sun and Moon are aligned opposite each other, the solar energy in Pingala becomes more dominant, driving action, creativity, and outward expression.”

Radha had always been affected by the lunar cycles. On full moon nights, she felt an overwhelming surge of energy, often struggling to sleep. After learning from Bhog about the influence of the Moon on her Ida and Pingala, she decided to experiment. On the next full moon, she spent the evening practicing left nostril breathing, activating the Ida Nadi to counterbalance the dominant solar energy of Pingala. To her surprise, she felt calmer, more at peace, and slept soundly that night.

Bhog then spoke of astrology's broader influence. "It is not only the Moon and Sun that impact the Swaras, but also other celestial bodies. For example, during astrological events like Mercury Retrograde, communication and mental clarity often suffer. This is because the flow of prana through Ida and Pingala may become disrupted, leading to imbalances in our energy and mind. By practicing alternate nostril breathing during these times, you can help restore balance and ease the effects of these cosmic influences."

Ravi, always full of questions, leaned forward. "Bhog, does this mean that the planets can directly affect how we breathe? Like, could the position of the planets in our birth chart affect which Swara is dominant?"

Bhog smiled at Ravi's enthusiasm. "May be, Ravi. Certain astrological signs and planetary alignments can influence which energy is more dominant in an individual. For instance, those with strong placements in water signs — like Cancer, Scorpio, and Pisces — might have a more active Ida Nadi, making them more receptive and emotionally sensitive. On the other hand, fire signs — such as Aries, Leo, and Sagittarius — might resonate more with Pingala, giving them a more active, energetic nature."

Ravi, born under the fiery sign of Leo, had always felt an intense, burning energy inside him. He was quick to act, often impulsive, and sometimes struggled with calming himself down. After learning about his natural alignment with Pingala energy, he decided to focus on Ida-activating practices to bring balance into his life. He began incorporating more left nostril breathing and cooling practices into his routine, and over time, Ravi found himself feeling calmer, more focused, and better able to channel his natural energy into productive pursuits.

Bhog then shifted the conversation to the influence of celestial events like eclipses. “During powerful astrological events such as solar and lunar eclipses, the energy flow through the nadis can be amplified or blocked. For example, during a solar eclipse, when the Moon blocks the Sun’s rays, the solar energy in Pingala can be temporarily diminished. This can lead to feelings of lethargy or confusion. Similarly, during a lunar eclipse, the flow of Ida may be disrupted, affecting our emotional state. Being mindful of these shifts and adjusting your practices accordingly can help maintain balance.”

Anika, who had often felt unsettled during eclipses, asked, “Bhog, how can we best manage our energy during these times?”

Bhog replied with his usual wisdom. “Anika, during eclipses, it’s important to stay grounded and balanced. You can practice both alternate nostril breathing and grounding asanas to help harmonize the flow of energy. Meditation during these times can also be powerful, allowing you to align with the cosmic forces rather than resist them.”

Anika had always felt anxious during eclipses, unsure of why her energy seemed to waver. After Bhog’s teachings, she began to view these celestial events not as disruptions but as opportunities for deep spiritual practice. During the next lunar eclipse, she spent time meditating and practicing alternate nostril breathing, bringing balance to both Ida and Pingala. Instead of feeling anxious, she felt a deep sense of connection to the universe, as though she had tapped into a higher energy flowing through the cosmos.

Bhog then concluded the lesson by speaking about the central nadi, Sushumna. “The ultimate goal of these practices is not just to balance Ida and Pingala, but to activate the central nadi, Sushumna, which leads to spiritual awakening. While astrology can influence the flow of Ida and Pingala, the path to Sushumna is one of deep meditation and awareness. Certain astrological alignments, like the rare conjunctions of Jupiter and Saturn, are believed to offer powerful opportunities for spiritual growth, as they create cosmic conditions that facilitate the flow of energy through Sushumna."

The villagers listened intently, absorbing the depth of Bhog's wisdom. They realized that the connection between astrology and Swara Yoga was not just an intellectual understanding but a way of living in harmony with the universe itself. As the echoes of Bhog's discourse fade into the stillness of the surrounding landscape, a moment of contemplative silence ensues. In this sacred pause, each individual reflects on the wisdom imparted by Bhog, recognizing the transformative power of self-awareness and spiritual awakening.

Mudras

The village awakened to the first light of dawn, a tranquil setting surrounded by lush fields and serene landscapes. The air was filled with the rhythmic sounds of nature, setting the stage for the unfolding of a remarkable day. In the heart of the village, a large banyan tree stood tall, its branches offering shade to the gathering people who assembled there daily for discussions and discourse.

On this particular morning, Bhog, known for his profound wisdom, took his customary seat under the ancient banyan tree. The people, eager to absorb his teachings, gathered around him in a semi-circle. As the gentle breeze carried the sweet fragrance of blooming flowers, Bhog began to speak, his words resonating with ancient wisdom.

"Dear people," Bhog addressed the attentive audience, "today, let us delve into the realm of mudras in yoga. Mudras are sacred gestures or seals that hold the power to harmonize the flow of prana, the life force that animates us. As we explore the significance of these gestures, we gain insights into the subtle connection between our bodies, minds, and the cosmic energies that surround us."

The discourse unfolded, with Bhog elucidating the essence of mudras and their role in maintaining the delicate balance of the five elements within the human body. He delved into the intricate connection between the fingers and the elements, painting a vivid picture of how the thumb, index finger, middle finger, ring finger, and pinky finger symbolized the elements of fire, air, space, earth, and water, respectively.

With each word, Bhog guided the people through the intricate web of pranas, explaining how these vital life energies manifest in the form of Apana, Samana, Prana, Vyana, and Udana. The people listened intently, absorbing the ancient wisdom that unfolded beneath the banyan tree.

As Bhog continued his discourse, he unveiled the secrets of hasta mudras — hand gestures that served as bridges between the individual and the divine. Anjali Mudra, Dhyana Mudra, Vayu Mudra, and an array of other mudras were unveiled, each with its unique purpose and benefits. Bhog emphasized how these mudras, when practiced with mindfulness, could bring about profound transformations in one's well-being.

Bhog continued his discourse in detail as below.

Hasta Mudras

"Mudras, or gestures and seals, are essential practices in yoga that help regulate the flow of prana (life force) within the body. Through specific hand movements, known as **hasta mudras**, body postures (kaya), or consciousness-focused gestures (chitta), prana is directed to different parts of the body. Ayurveda connects these gestures with balancing the five elements — fire, air, space, earth, and water — that exist in the body, with each finger representing a specific element. When these elements are in balance, the body functions harmoniously; any imbalance can lead to illness or discomfort.

In mudra practice, we manipulate the flow of prana by adjusting the fingers, which correspond to these elements:

- **Thumb**: Fire
- **Index finger**: Air
- **Middle finger**: Space
- **Ring finger**: Earth
- **Pinky finger**: Water

The practice of mudras also aids in balancing the body's five pranas:

1. **Apana**: Governs elimination processes.
2. **Samana**: Regulates digestion and metabolism.
3. **Prana**: Supports the heart and respiration.
4. **Vyana**: Facilitates circulation and movement.
5. **Udana**: Governs speech, thought, and upper-body actions."

Bhog started with **Anjali Mudra**, pressing his palms together at his chest. "This gesture," Bhog explained, "cultivates reverence, gratitude, and inner balance. It unites the left and right hemispheres of the brain, helping you connect to the divine and to each other."

Maya, known for her nurturing spirit, placed her hands in Anjali Mudra and felt a wave of peaceful energy wash over her. Even Aryan, usually restless, followed along, feeling a rare stillness settle within him. The simplicity of the gesture resonated deeply, as though the act of joining hands created an instant connection with the universe.

Bhog then transitioned to **Dhyana Mudra**, resting his hands on his lap with his right hand atop the left and thumbs touching. "This mudra," he said, "is for deep meditation. It sharpens focus and invites inner stillness."

The villagers practiced in silence, their breath deepening with each passing moment. Amara, often busy with her responsibilities, felt her usually active mind quiet as she entered a state of rare calm. Kartik, too, found his often-tensed body relaxing into the moment.

Next, Bhog demonstrated **Vayu Mudra**, folding his index finger and pressing it gently with his thumb. "This gesture," he explained, "balances the air element in your body. It helps to calm anxiety and bring steadiness when you feel scattered."

Kartik, who often fidgeted, immediately noticed a change in his body's energy. The tension in his shoulders eased, and his mind, usually filled with worries, calmed. He looked at Bhog in quiet wonder, amazed at how such a simple gesture could create such a profound shift.

Moving on, Bhog introduced **Shunya Mudra**, pressing his middle finger with the thumb. "This mudra balances the space element within you and helps alleviate ear issues while bringing mental clarity."

Amara, who often found herself overwhelmed by the endless tasks of village life, practiced the mudra and felt a subtle sense of lightness within her mind, as though a weight had been lifted. The fog of stress that had clouded her thoughts seemed to dissipate, leaving behind clarity and focus.

Next, Bhog guided them into **Prithvi Mudra**, touching the thumb and ring finger together. “This mudra grounds you,” he said, “balancing the Earth element and promoting stability and endurance.”

Amara, often feeling overwhelmed by the demands of her daily life, sensed a deep connection to the earth as she practiced the mudra. She felt as though the ground beneath her was supporting her in a way she hadn’t noticed before, offering her strength and stability.

Bhog then introduced **Varuna Mudra**, where he touched the tips of his thumb and little finger together. “This gesture balances water in the body, helping with detoxification and emotional equilibrium.”

As the villagers practiced, they felt an emotional release. Anika, who often carried the worries of her family, felt a lightness, as though her emotions were more in balance, her heart unburdened.

Bhog demonstrated **Shakti Mudra**, folding his thumb under his fingers and connecting his ring and little fingers with both hands. “This mudra,” he explained, “balances your masculine and feminine energies, bringing vitality and harmony to your relationships.”

Amara practiced the mudra and felt a deep sense of alignment within herself. Aryan, though young, experienced a surge of energy that left him feeling invigorated, as if the gesture had awakened something powerful within.

Next was **Hakini Mudra**, where Bhog brought his fingertips together. “This mudra harmonizes your brain hemispheres and enhances focus, memory, and concentration.”

Aryan, who often struggled with his schoolwork, found his mind unusually clear and focused. Amara, too, noticed her thoughts sharpening, the usual distractions fading away.

Bhog introduced **Prana Mudra**, touching the tips of his thumb, ring, and little fingers. “This is the mudra of life force,” he said. “It boosts your energy and strengthens your immune system.”

Kartik, who had felt fatigued from the hard work of the fields, practiced the mudra and immediately sensed a revitalizing energy flowing through him. Aryan, normally brimming with excess energy, found himself more centered and balanced.

Bhog demonstrated **Apana Mudra**, where he touched his thumb, middle, and ring fingers together. “This mudra supports detoxification and aids digestion, helping balance the downward flow of energy.”

Anika, mindful of her health, practiced the mudra and felt a sense of relief, as though her body was flushing out impurities. She breathed deeply, feeling lighter and more in tune with her body’s needs.

Next came **Poorna Mudra**, where Bhog joined his thumb and little fingers. “This is the mudra of completeness,” he said, “promoting spiritual awareness and a sense of inner wholeness.”

The villagers practiced the mudra and felt a profound connection to themselves and the world around them. Amara, who had long sought inner peace, found herself enveloped in a sense of completeness and calm.

Bhog introduced **Gyana Mudra** and **Jnana Mudra**, connecting the thumb and index finger to form a circle. “These mudras stimulate focus and wisdom,” he explained. “They open the mind to knowledge and universal understanding.”

Yash, who often sought answers to life's mysteries, felt his thoughts clear. Aryan, struggling with concentration, found his mind sharper, as though the fog had lifted.

Bhog then guided them through **Adi Mudra** and **Chinmaya Mudra**, explaining how they calm the mind, balance awareness, and support deep meditation. Aryan, usually full of restless energy, found himself calm and steady, his racing thoughts finally quieted.

Next came **Yoni Mudra**, which Bhog explained connects you to the feminine energy of creation. As the villagers practiced, they felt grounded and introspective. Maya felt a deep connection to her inner world, the external stresses fading away.

Finally, Bhog introduced **Hridaya Mudra**, activating the heart chakra. "This mudra enhances emotional well-being, promoting self-love and compassion," Bhog said.

The villagers practiced in silence, their hearts opening as they connected to their deepest selves. Anika, often struggling with self-doubt, felt a warm wave of self-compassion wash over her, filling her heart with love.

As the session drew to a close, Bhog reminded the villagers to practice with care and respect for their bodies. He offered guidance on each mudra, emphasizing the importance of gentle practice and awareness of any discomfort.

"Remember," Bhog said, "these mudras are powerful tools, but they must be used wisely. Listen to your body, practice with intention, and allow the energy to flow naturally."

The villagers, filled with a newfound sense of peace, gratitude, and balance, left the banyan tree that day, carrying with them the transformative power of the **Hasta Mudras**. With each gesture, they knew they were tapping into the vast energy within, ready to face the challenges of life with grace and harmony.

Mana Mudras in Yoga

Next morning, the golden light of dawn filtered through the trees, casting a warm glow over the village. The villagers, as always, gathered beneath the shade of the ancient banyan tree, eager to learn from Bhog. The air was fresh, filled with the chirping of birds and the scent of dew. Today, however, there was an extra sense of anticipation, for Bhog had promised to take them deeper into the mystical world of **Mana Mudras**.

Kalpana, always eager to absorb new teachings, sat at the front of the group alongside Aryan, the restless young boy who had recently found peace through Bhog's lessons. Yash, Ravi, and Amara were also present, their faces filled with curiosity as Bhog prepared to guide them through the sacred gestures of the head, which held the power to unlock hidden realms of consciousness.

Bhog's gentle smile calmed the gathering as he began, "Dear ones, today we will dive into the world of **Mana Mudras**, gestures that transcend the physical and awaken the mind to higher realms. These mudras are keys to unlocking the deeper layers of your consciousness. Through these practices, we can harmonize the body, mind, and spirit."

Bhog started with the **Shambhavi Mudra**, gently closing his eyes and focusing on the space between his eyebrows. "This mudra," he explained, "opens the Ajna chakra, or third eye. It helps you see beyond the material world and awakens your intuition."

Bhog cautioned, "This mudra enhances focus, but if you strain your eyes or feel tension in your forehead, stop. Ease into it and avoid pushing beyond what feels comfortable."

Kalpana, who often struggled with overwhelming thoughts, followed Bhog's lead. As she directed her gaze upward, she felt an inner calm wash over her. Even Aryan, known for his restless energy, found a deep sense of focus as he practiced the mudra.

Bhog smiled at Aryan's newfound concentration and said, "When your thoughts settle, you can see the truth more clearly."

Next, Bhog introduced **Nasikagra Drishti**, the nose-tip gazing mudra. He turned to Aryan with a playful grin, "This one is perfect for calming a wandering mind."

He advised, "While this mudra calms the mind, excessive practice can strain the eyes. Remember to rest if you feel discomfort."

Aryan eagerly tried the mudra, fixing his gaze on the tip of his nose. As his focus sharpened, his usual scattered thoughts quieted, replaced by a peaceful stillness. The villagers, watching Aryan's transformation, followed suit, each feeling a sense of calm take over.

"Balance is key," Bhog reminded them. "This mudra draws scattered energy inward, centering the mind."

Moving on to more advanced techniques, Bhog demonstrated **Khechari Mudra**, rolling his tongue back toward the nasal cavity. He explained, "This mudra is deeply spiritual and not for everyone just yet. It requires time and dedication, but it awakens profound spiritual states and brings control over the senses."

Bhog warned, "This advanced mudra should only be attempted with a teacher's guidance. Forcing it can cause strain or injury."

Amara, always fascinated by Bhog's teachings, observed closely but knew this was a practice for the future. Amara, intrigued by the idea of controlling the body and mind in such a way, made a mental note to try this mudra once she had gained more experience.

Bhog then led the group into **Kaki Mudra**, gently pursing his lips like a crow's beak and taking slow, deliberate breaths. "This mudra," he said, "sharpens focus and clears confusion. It is perfect for those moments when anxiety clouds the mind."

Bhog added, "This mudra is safe for most, but if you feel short of breath, stop and breathe naturally."

Amara, who had been worried about the future, practiced the gesture and immediately felt her tension ease. For the first time in days, a sense of calm settled over her.

"Breathe deeply and slowly," Bhog instructed, "and let the clarity come."

Bhog then introduced **Bhujangini Mudra**, where they simulated drinking air like water, gulping it into their stomachs. "This mudra stimulates the digestive system and energizes the voice," he explained.

He cautioned "This can be powerful for digestion, but those with respiratory or heart conditions should avoid holding the breath for too long."

Aryan, always eager for something physical, found this mudra particularly fun, making exaggerated sounds as he practiced. The villagers, though more restrained, felt their lungs expanding and their bodies filling with energy.

Next came **Bhoochari Mudra**, focusing on the earth element. Bhog instructed them to form a loose fist with their right hand and place it near their mouths, gazing at their little fingers.

"This mudra," Bhog said, "grounds you. It aligns you with the earth, bringing stability."

Bhog reminded them, "If you have spine or neck issues, practice with care. Adjust your posture if discomfort arises."

Kartik, who often felt overwhelmed by his responsibilities, noticed how this mudra made him feel more rooted, more present. The worries that usually weighed him down seemed to lighten.

Raising their heads toward the sky, Bhog introduced **Akashi Mudra**, instructing the villagers to breathe deeply as they gazed upward. “This mudra opens you to the vastness of the universe,” Bhog explained. “It brings awareness to the space within and around you.”

Bhog cautioned, “Do not perform this if you have high blood pressure or suffer from dizziness. Always listen to your body.”

As they practiced, the villagers felt their awareness expand, stretching beyond their bodies. Amara felt a sense of lightness as her worries drifted away, merging with the vast blue sky above.

The next practice was **Shanmukhi Mudra**, where Bhog guided the villagers to close their ears, eyes, and mouth with their fingers. “By blocking the senses, you turn inward,” he said. “This mudra brings you into deep inner silence, where you can hear the voice of your true self.”

As the villagers sat in profound silence, Aryan felt a peace he had never experienced before. Without the noise of the outside world, he was able to connect with a deeper part of himself.

Finally, Bhog introduced **Unmani Mudra**, or the “State of No Mind.” “This mudra slows down the mind, taking you beyond thoughts,” he said softly. “It brings you into a state of pure being.”

Bhog advised, “Avoid both of these mudras if you have respiratory issues or if you feel overwhelmed by the silence. Let stillness come naturally, without force.”

As they practiced, Anika felt herself letting go of the constant stream of thoughts. For the first time, she experienced what Bhog had often spoken about — a state where the mind was quiet, and only pure awareness remained.

As the session came to a close, the villagers opened their eyes, feeling more connected to themselves and each other. Bhog's teachings had left an indelible mark on their hearts and minds.

As the sun climbed higher into the sky, the villagers dispersed, each carrying the wisdom of these sacred gestures.

Yoga Asanas

As the golden light of dawn cast a soft glow over the village, the villagers gathered once again beneath the ancient banyan tree, their hearts filled with anticipation. Bhog, standing at the center, radiated serenity as he prepared to guide them through a transformative session of Yoga Asanas. Among the group were Ravi, Yash, Amara, Kartik, and the ever-curious Kalpana and Maya, each eager to deepen their understanding of yoga's power.

Bhog's calm presence was reassuring as he began to speak. "Today, dear ones," he said, his voice gentle yet filled with purpose, "we will journey through the fundamentals of yoga asanas. These postures are more than mere physical movements; they are gateways to balance, strength, and inner peace. Also, do these asanas as per your convenience, take rest or skip the asanas if you feel any discomfort, it's just for learning on how to do these asanas and how they contribute your overall well being."

Yash, seated at the front, looked toward Ravi with a gleam in his eyes. "I've been waiting for this," Yash whispered, his excitement barely contained. Ravi smiled, equally eager to begin.

Surya Namaskar (Basic) Bhog initiated the practice with **Surya Namaskar (Sun Salutation)**, the sacred sequence that honors the rising sun. The villagers stood tall in **Pranamasana (Prayer Pose)**, hands pressed together at their hearts. As Bhog's voice guided them, they transitioned through each movement, synchronizing their breath with the flowing postures.

Amara, always deeply connected to her body, moved gracefully, her breath steady as she followed Bhog's guidance. Kalpana, standing beside her, tried her best to keep up, her small form mirroring the movements of those around her.

With each transition — **Hastauttanasana (Raised Arms Pose)**, **Hasta Padasana (Hand to Foot Pose)**, and **Ashwa Sanchalanasana (Equestrian Pose)** — the villagers felt a deep connection to the earth and sky, their bodies stretching and strengthening in unison.

Bhog's Gentle Guidance "Feel the energy of the rising sun fill your bodies," Bhog encouraged. "Surya Namaskar is not just a physical practice but a celebration of life, a way to align our inner rhythms with the natural world."

As the villagers moved into **Bhujangasana (Cobra Pose)** and finally into **Parvatasana (Mountain Pose)**, Bhog reminded them to breathe deeply, to ground themselves in the strength of the earth beneath their feet. Even Kartik, who often found it hard to remain still, felt the calming effect of the practice.

After completing several rounds of the sequence, Bhog paused, allowing the villagers to reflect on the energy now coursing through their bodies.

"Surya Namaskar strengthens your muscles, increases flexibility, and promotes cardiovascular health," he explained. "But most importantly, it revitalizes your spirit."

Basic Yoga Asanas Bhog then led the group into a series of **basic asanas**, carefully explaining each posture and its benefits. He began with **Tadasana (Mountain Pose)**, where the villagers stood tall, feet together, arms reaching toward the sky.

"**Tadasana**," Bhog said, "is the foundation of all standing poses. It improves posture, strengthens the legs, and brings a sense of stability to both body and mind."

Yash, eager to prove his strength, stood as tall as he could, his chest puffed out. Amara, noticing his enthusiasm, smiled and whispered, "Balance your breath, Yash. That's where the real strength comes from."

Next, Bhog guided them into **Adho Mukha Svanasana (Downward-Facing Dog)**, pressing their hands into the earth and lifting their hips toward the sky. "This asana stretches the entire body," Bhog explained. "It brings relief to the spine and strengthens the arms and legs."

As they moved through **Virabhadrasana I (Warrior I)** and **Virabhadrasana II (Warrior II)**, the group found their grounding. Bhog spoke of the inner strength required for these warrior poses, a strength not just of the body but of the spirit.

"Hold your ground, like a warrior in life," Bhog said, his voice steady. "These asanas open the chest, build inner courage, and help you find balance amidst the challenges of life."

Ravi, always the competitive one, felt the burn in his legs but held the pose, inspired by Bhog's words. Maya, wobbling at first in **Vrikshasana (Tree Pose)**, giggled as she found her balance, raising her arms above her head like the branches of a tree.

"**Vrikshasana** teaches us to be rooted yet flexible," Bhog explained. "In life, we face challenges, but with focus and breath, we remain grounded."

Seated Poses and Relaxation The group then moved to the ground, following Bhog's lead into **Balasana (Child's Pose)**. As they folded forward, foreheads touching the earth, Bhog's voice softened.

"This is a place of rest, where we reconnect with our breath," he said. "It relaxes the spine and calms the nervous system."

Even Ravi, who usually preferred more dynamic poses, sighed in relief as he sank into the posture, feeling the tension in his body melt away.

Bhog guided them into **Paschimottanasana (Seated Forward Bend)** next. As the villagers reached toward their toes, Bhog reminded them to breathe deeply, feeling the stretch in their spines and hamstrings.

"**Paschimottanasana** stretches the body and calms the mind," Bhog explained. "It's also wonderful for improving digestion."

Amara, feeling the deep stretch in her back, closed her eyes, embracing the calm that came with each breath.

The Final Relaxation Finally, Bhog guided the villagers into **Savasana (Corpse Pose)**, the ultimate posture of relaxation. As they lay on their backs, eyes closed, Bhog encouraged them to surrender completely to the stillness.

"**Savasana** allows the mind and body to integrate the benefits of your practice," Bhog said, his voice gentle. "It promotes deep relaxation and reduces stress."

As they rested in Savasana, the warmth of the sun on their skin, the villagers felt a profound sense of peace. Bhog's teachings had once again filled them with a renewed sense of balance and clarity.

As the session came to an end, Bhog's gaze rested on each of them with deep gratitude. "Yoga is not just about the physical postures," he reminded them. "It is about finding harmony within ourselves and with the world around us."

With a collective "Om," the session concluded, the sound resonating through the air like a gentle ripple across the surface of a still pond. The villagers rose from their mats, their bodies and spirits rejuvenated, ready to carry the wisdom of Bhog's teachings into their daily lives.

As they dispersed, Ravi nudged Yash with a grin. "Told you today would be amazing."

Yash smiled back; his heart full of the quiet strength that only Bhog's guidance could instill. Amara, Kartik, Radha, and the others walked back to the village, the warmth of the morning sun on their faces, knowing they had once again touched the essence of yoga — a balance between body, mind, and spirit.

Pranayamas

The morning sun gently illuminated the village as the people gathered once more beneath the ancient banyan tree. Bhog stood at the center, radiating calm and wisdom. Today, the villagers — Ravi, Amara, Kartik, Radha, and even the youngest, Kalpana and Maya — were filled with anticipation. They had all heard Bhog speak of the profound power of Pranayama, and now, they were eager to dive deeper into the practice that promised not just physical vitality but spiritual connection.

As everyone settled in, Ravi, always full of energy, nudged his younger cousin Yash. "Today's going to be amazing," he whispered. Yash nodded; a bit distracted but curious. Amara, sitting next to them, smiled softly. She had been exploring yoga for years now but felt she was only beginning to scratch the surface. Kartik, Radha, and the elder Anika were all present as well, eager to learn more about this ancient breath control technique that Bhog had promised would change their understanding of life.

Bhog began with his usual calm authority. “Dear ones, today, we embark on the journey of Pranayama — the mastery of breath. It is through the control of our breath that we connect body, mind, and spirit, and find true harmony within ourselves.”

The group listened attentively. Even the youngest, Kalpana and Maya, sat quietly, captivated by Bhog’s gentle but powerful presence. Amara raised a hand, “Bhog, how does breath connect us to the spirit? I’ve always felt it’s just something we do, not something we can control.”

Bhog smiled. “Ah, Amara, the breath is more than just the act of drawing in air. It is the life force — prana — that sustains us. By controlling our breath, we control our life energy, and that, dear ones, is the key to true balance.”

Guidelines for Pranayama

Bhog continued by sharing the guidelines for practicing Pranayama. “First,” he said, “a strong foundation in asanas is essential. Pranayama should always be approached with care and under the guidance of a teacher.” He emphasized the importance of self-discipline and mindful nourishment, encouraging the group to keep their minds and bodies pure through simple foods offered to the divine.

Ravi, ever inquisitive, leaned forward. “But Bhog, why is it so important to keep the body light for pranayama?”

Bhog answered thoughtfully, “When the body is weighed down by impure food or distractions, the mind becomes clouded, and the prana cannot flow freely. A light body allows the breath to move with ease, bringing balance and peace to the mind."

Cleansing the Nadis

Bhog then introduced the concept of **nadi shodhana**, or cleansing the energy channels. "The nadis are the pathways through which prana flows," he explained. "But over time, impurities block these channels. Through pranayama, particularly alternate nostril breathing — **Anuloma Viloma** — we can cleanse the nadis and allow prana to flow smoothly."

Amara and Kartik followed Bhog's demonstration, gently closing one nostril and inhaling through the other, switching sides as instructed. They could feel a subtle change — a sense of lightness and clarity spreading through their bodies.

"Bhog," Kartik asked, "how do we know when our nadis are truly cleansed?"

Bhog smiled gently. "You will know, Kartik. The body will feel lighter, the mind more focused, and the breath will flow effortlessly. When your nadis are clear, you will feel a deep sense of balance and peace."

Procedure for Pranayama

As the villagers practiced their breathing, Bhog guided them through the correct procedure for Pranayama. Sitting in **Padmasana** (Lotus Pose), he demonstrated how to seal one nostril with the thumb and breathe slowly through the other. "Inhale deeply," he instructed, "filling your belly with air. Then, switch nostrils and exhale gently."

Ravi, always eager to test his limits, held his breath longer than the others, trying to push himself. Bhog noticed and gently corrected him. "Patience, Ravi. Pranayama is not a race. Breath control comes with time, and it must be gentle. Listen to your body."

Even Yash, who often struggled to stay focused, found himself falling into the rhythm of the breath, his usually restless energy calming down.

Benefits of Pranayama

As they practiced, Bhog spoke of the many benefits of pranayama. "Pranayama, when done correctly, purifies the body of toxins, strengthens the lungs, and balances the energies within. It prepares the mind for meditation and creates harmony in the body."

Radha, always nurturing and mindful of her health, asked, "Bhog, does pranayama help with stress and emotional well-being too?"

Bhog nodded. "Indeed, Radha. By calming the breath, we calm the mind. Regular practice of pranayama reduces anxiety, alleviates stress, and brings mental clarity. It is a tool for physical health as well as emotional and spiritual balance."

Precautions and Contraindications

The atmosphere shifted as Bhog's tone grew more serious. "But remember, dear ones, pranayama is a powerful tool, and like all powerful tools, it must be used with care." He warned them against overextending their breath, especially in the beginning. "Holding the breath too long can lead to dizziness or strain. Always listen to your body. If you feel discomfort, stop and breathe naturally."

He also spoke to those with health concerns. "If you have respiratory issues, high blood pressure, or heart conditions, it's important to modify the practice. Always consult a teacher before attempting advanced techniques."

Kalpana, the youngest, looked up with wide eyes. “Bhog, can I do it too, or is it too hard for me?”

Bhog smiled warmly at her. “You can certainly try, little one, but gently. For now, just focus on breathing slowly and calmly. The more you practice, the more you'll grow into it.”

As the session came to a close, the villagers felt a deep sense of calm and clarity. Amara looked over at Ravi, who was surprisingly quiet for once, fully immersed in the experience. Kartik stretched his legs and smiled, feeling lighter and more at ease.

Bhog's final words lingered in the air like the gentle breeze. “Pranayama is not just about controlling the breath. It is the bridge between body and spirit. It connects us to the divine and helps us master our inner selves.”

The villagers, filled with a newfound sense of harmony, slowly made their way home, their hearts lighter, their minds clearer. As they left, the soft rustling of the banyan tree seemed to echo Bhog's wisdom — a reminder that through the breath, they could find not only balance in life but also a deeper connection to their true selves.

Six intense kriyas to purify the body

Beneath the ancient banyan tree, the villagers had gathered once again for their daily teachings with Bhog. Today, Bhog had planned to introduce the six intense kriyas, powerful techniques used to purify the body, mind, and spirit.

Ravi, the 17-year-old full of energy and curiosity, sat close to the front, his eyes wide with anticipation. He had always been fascinated by Bhog's teachings, but this morning, something seemed different. Sitting next to him was his younger cousin Yash, who was just as eager to learn but sometimes found himself easily distracted.

Amara, the 25-year-old creative spirit, sat beside Kartik, the 45-year-old who had been seeking balance between his work and family. They all listened closely as Bhog began.

"Today, dear ones," Bhog started, his voice calm but filled with purpose, "we will delve into the six kriyas — powerful cleansing techniques that will not only purify the body but also sharpen the mind and uplift the spirit."

Anika, now 60 and deeply committed to her spiritual journey, leaned forward with interest. She had heard of these kriyas before but had never practiced them. Meanwhile, Radha, nurturing and always concerned with relationships, smiled gently as Kalpana and Maya, the youngest at 9 and 7, whispered quietly among themselves. They were too young to practice, but they loved hearing the stories.

Bhog started with **Dhauti**, explaining the cloth-cleaning method. Amara raised her hand. "Bhog, that sounds difficult! Swallowing a cloth… Is it safe?"

Bhog nodded, his eyes filled with understanding. "Yes, it can be challenging, and that's why it must only be done under careful guidance, Amara. It cleanses the stomach of toxins, but for most of us, simpler versions of this practice, like water cleansing, are just as beneficial."

Next, Bhog spoke of **Basti**, the ancient form of internal cleansing using water. Kartik, who was always practical, asked, "But how does this help our everyday life, Bhog? I understand it's for purification, but when would one need to practice something like Basti?"

Bhog smiled warmly. "Basti is a deep cleanse, Kartik. It's not something we do every day. It balances the doshas — vata, pitta, and kapha — removing impurities. Think of it as a reset button for the body. But yes, it's not for everyone to practice casually."

Ravi, always eager for something adventurous, leaned in when Bhog described **Neti** — the practice of passing a string through the nose and out through the mouth. "Bhog, can I try this one? It sounds like a challenge!"

Before Bhog could answer, Anika gently laughed. "Ravi, perhaps you should wait a little. It might be better to start with something simpler."

Bhog chuckled. "Anika is right, Ravi. Neti, like all these kriyas, requires patience and practice. It clears the nasal passages and sharpens your vision, but it's not something to rush into."

As Bhog described **Trataka**, the gazing meditation, Yash, who had trouble focusing, perked up. "I think I could do that one, Bhog. I'm always getting distracted... Will this help?"

"Absolutely, Yash," Bhog said kindly. "Trataka strengthens your concentration. By focusing on a single point until your eyes water, you clear mental distractions. It's perfect for building focus."

The room fell quiet as Bhog introduced **Nauli**, the kriya that involved rolling the stomach muscles from side to side. Radha, always attentive to everyone's well-being, raised a concerned hand. "Bhog, this sounds difficult. Should we all be trying this?"

Bhog's voice softened. "Nauli is powerful, but it's also advanced. It's a tool for deepening digestion and balancing the body's internal fire. For most of you, breathing exercises and gentle movements will suffice for now."

Finally, Bhog explained **Kapala Bhati**, the practice of forceful exhalations. Kalpana, the youngest, looked confused. "Bhog, why would you want to breathe like a blacksmith's bellows?"

Everyone smiled as Bhog bent down to her level. “Ah, little one, it’s a way to get rid of excess phlegm and toxins from the body. Like cleaning out cobwebs in a house, it clears the mind and body.”

The villagers sat in quiet contemplation as Bhog’s teachings sank in. Ravi, always full of questions, couldn’t resist asking one more. “Bhog, how do we know when to use these kriyas? When is the right time?”

Bhog gazed at Ravi, then at the others. “These kriyas, Ravi, are not everyday practices. They are powerful tools, to be used when the body needs deep cleansing — when we feel heavy, sluggish, or stuck in our progress. And always, always with guidance. For now, focus on your asanas and pranayama. In time, you’ll know when it’s right to explore the kriyas.”

The sun had risen higher in the sky as Bhog concluded the lesson. “Remember, dear ones, these kriyas are sacred practices, and they must be done with care and respect for the body. Always practice with patience and mindfulness.”

As the villagers began to disperse, Amara turned to Kartik. “I think I’ll start with something gentle, maybe Trataka. You?”

Kartik nodded. “I’ll stick to pranayama for now. But it’s good to know these practices exist when we need them.”

Yash tugged at Ravi’s sleeve. “I bet I could beat you at Trataka.”

Ravi grinned. “You’re on!”

As the group walked away, their hearts lighter with new knowledge, the banyan tree stood tall, its leaves whispering the timeless wisdom that Bhog had shared with them all.

As the session ended, the villagers sat in quiet contemplation. They had learned much about the power of kriyas, but Bhog’s final words resonated most deepl "These six kriyas purify the body, yes — but more importantly, they purify the mind and soul. Through them, we prepare ourselves to walk the path of truth, to connect with the divine, and to live in harmony with all that is."

The people, filled with gratitude, slowly rose from their mats. The sun was now higher in the sky, casting a warm, golden light on the banyan tree and the village below. As they dispersed, they carried with them not just the techniques of the kriyas, but the deeper wisdom of Bhog's teachings — knowing that the path to purity is a journey of body, mind, and spirit, walked one breath at a time.

Chapter 3

Stages of our Mind and Healing of Body through Mind

In the evening, the villagers gathered under the soft glow of lantern light as Bhog prepared to share his insights. WIth a calm demeanor and an aura of tranquility, Bhog began to unravel the profound connection between thoughts, emotions, and the well-being of the self.

Amara, feeling a deep resonance with the topic, sat at the front, while Aryan, always full of questions, sat beside her, his curiosity already stirred. The people of the village listened intently as Bhog's voice carried the weight of introspection.

"In our pursuit of a better life, we unknowingly harm ourselves," Bhog began, his gaze sweeping across the attentive villagers. "The victim and the killer are one and the same — it's us, ourselves."

The villagers looked at one another, trying to grasp the depth of his words. Ravi, who had often struggled with feelings of guilt for not meeting societal expectations, leaned forward, eager to understand Bhog's message.

Bhog continued, delving into the consequences of attachment to outcomes. "Whenever we attach ourselves to the fruits of our actions, we weaken an essential life force within us. The moment we make our happiness dependent on results, we silently kill our joy."

Amara, who had often placed pressure on herself to meet expectations in her work and relationships, felt a pang of recognition. She realized how often she had attached her worth to success or acknowledgment from others. Bhog's words illuminated a truth she had been avoiding.

"Our thoughts and emotions shape both the physical and subtle aspects of our being," Bhog said softly, drawing a connection between the divine trinity and the self. "God resides within us, working based on the instructions we send. Brahma, Vishnu, and Mahesh — the creator, the manager, and the destroyer — all exist within us, shaping our reality according to our thoughts."

Aryan, always fascinated by stories of gods and creation, raised his hand. "So, Bhog, does that mean our thoughts are like commands to the gods inside us?"

Bhog nodded, smiling at Aryan's insight. "Yes, Aryan. Every thought, every emotion, sends a signal to the divine forces within us. When we dwell on anger, guilt, or jealousy, we invite destruction. But when we cultivate joy, love, and gratitude, we strengthen our life force."

Amara, reflecting on Bhog's words, raised her hand. "But what about when we face negative emotions? How can we stop them from controlling us?"

Bhog's gaze softened. "We cannot always control external events, but we can control our response. When we feel anger, guilt, or jealousy, instead of attaching to those emotions, we can observe them mindfully and let them pass. By doing so, we stop the cycle of self-sabotage."

Kartik, who had recently dealt with personal setbacks, felt a deep connection to Bhog's teachings. He had spent countless hours worrying about the future, and now he understood how that worry had been weakening his spirit. "But how do we break this habit, Bhog?" Kartik asked.

Bhog smiled gently. “It begins with awareness. When we notice that we are attaching ourselves to an outcome or a negative emotion, we pause. We acknowledge the thought, but we do not let it consume us. We remind ourselves that our worth is not tied to external results but to our inner state of being.”

He added, “Every time we attach ourselves to an outcome — whether it's success, validation, or acknowledgment — we kill something inside ourselves. These attachments manifest as stress, anxiety, or even physical illness. But when we live mindfully and focus on the process rather than the outcome, we cultivate inner peace.”

Amara reflected on Bhog's words about duality, the interplay between thoughts and sounds. “So, Bhog, if our thoughts are powerful, does that mean we can consciously shape our emotions through mindful practices?”

“Absolutely,” Bhog replied. “Just as listening to a song can evoke emotions, we can choose thoughts that nurture positive feelings. It's the dualistic nature of Purush and Prakruti — our thoughts shape our bodies, and our bodies influence our thoughts. Mindfulness allows us to break the cycle of negative thinking and replace it with conscious, intentional living.”

Aryan, always quick to see the practical side of things, asked, “So, does that mean when we worry, we're basically giving the god inside us instructions to bring more problems?”

Bhog chuckled, nodding. “Yes, Aryan. When we worry, we do it mindfully, sending clear instructions to the divine within us. The more we focus on negative outcomes, the more likely those outcomes become. That's why it's essential to train our minds to focus on the positive, to live and love mindfully.”

AUM, Chakras and their significance in breathing

As the evening drew on, the villagers absorbed Bhog's teachings, reflecting on how their thoughts and emotions had been shaping their lives. They realized that they held the power to strengthen or weaken their own life force, depending on how they chose to think and feel.

Bhog added "The creator, the manager, and the destroyer all reside within us. It is up to us which force we empower through our thoughts and emotions. When we live mindfully, without attachment to outcomes, we cultivate the joy and strength that are our true nature.

Let me provide you with an important aspect of our Body, our breath, mind and the manifestation.

In Sanatana philosophy, "AUM" has an important significance, its known as "pranav" mantra. It itself represents the sounds of the universe and three deities, Brahma, Vishnu and Mahesh (Shiva). The vibration (reverberance) of AUM represents the full cycle of creation, preservation and destruction. The sound of Creation or Nature, we also know it as "Anahata Nada" the sound produced without striking or unstruck sound is like humming of AUM only.

This sound is generated by atoms of the universe vibrating at different frequencies.

AUM represents a full cycle of creation, preservation and destruction. The Aum symbol (ॐ) visually represents these three aspects: A (bottom curve), U (middle curve), M (upper curve), and the Bindu (dot) or the silent fourth state (Turiya) above the curves.

- The continuous chanting of Aum is believed to align an individual's consciousness with the cosmic vibrations, bringing about a sense of unity with the divine and the cyclical nature of existence. It is regarded as a symbol of the ultimate reality or Brahman, encompassing the entire spectrum of existence.

The Aum sound is a sacred syllable that encapsulates the cosmic processes of creation, preservation, and destruction. Chanting Aum is believed to connect individuals with the universal forces and the ultimate reality, fostering spiritual growth and a deeper understanding of the nature of existence.

“Aum” is a sacred spiritual icon in Hinduism, Buddhism, Jainism, and other Dharmic religions. It is considered a fundamental vibration or cosmic sound that represents the essence of the ultimate reality or consciousness. The sound “Aum” is associated with the creation, preservation, and destruction of the universe. Here’s how the Aum sound is connected to these aspects:

1. **A - Creation (Brahma):**

   – The first part of the Aum sound is “A,” representing the aspect of creation. It symbolizes the beginning, birth, or origin of all existence.

   – “A” is associated with Lord Brahma, the creator in Hinduism. It signifies the creative force and the unfolding of the universe.

2. **U - Preservation (Vishnu)**:

   – The second part of the Aum sound is “U,” representing the aspect of preservation. It symbolizes the sustaining and maintaining force in the universe.

   – “U” is associated with Lord Vishnu, the preserver in Hinduism. It signifies the enduring and nurturing qualities that help sustain the created universe.

3. **M - Destruction (Shiva):**

   - The third part of the Aum sound is "M," representing the aspect of destruction. It symbolizes the transformative and regenerative force in the cycle of existence.

   - "M" is associated with Lord Shiva, the destroyer and transformer in Hinduism. It signifies the process of dissolution, allowing for the renewal and recreation of the universe.

4. **Silence (Turiya):**

   - Beyond the three individual sounds, there is a fourth aspect, often represented by the silence that follows the chanting of Aum.

   - This silence is called "Turiya," representing the transcendent or the ultimate reality that goes beyond the cycles of creation, preservation, and destruction. It signifies the state of pure consciousness and unity.

One Single cycle of breath, inhalation, retention, exhalation, retention (repeat) represents the same thing happening in our own body where creation preservation and destruction happens as part of the same breath cycle (Praan vaayu), that's why the way we breathe defines our alignment with the overall cosmic nature of universe and the better aligned we are, the better our whole system works.

Now the way we think and respond to situations around us, we continuously keep giving our inner GOD instructions on what we really are expecting from our lives, our bodies, whatever we tell it, the same we get back, being the creator, manifestor, destroyer, it just accepts what we ask. In lieu of our stress, worries, anxieties, overthinking mostly keeps giving wrong instructions/asks/

expectations which ultimately leads to disorders/diseases in our mind and body.

The chanting of the "Aum" sound is believed to activate and resonate with various chakras, which are energy centers in the subtle body according to traditional Indian spiritual and yogic traditions. Different parts of the "Aum" sound are associated with different chakras. Here's a breakdown:

1. **A - Root Chakra (Muladhara):**
   - The "A" sound in Aum is associated with the Muladhara or the Root Chakra, located at the base of the spine.
   - Activation of the Root Chakra is believed to promote a sense of grounding, stability, and connection to the physical world.
2. **U - Naval/Sacral Chakra (Svadhishthana):**
   - The "U" sound is linked to the Svadhishthana or Sacral Chakra, situated in the lower abdomen.
   - Activation of the Sacral Chakra is associated with creativity, emotional balance, and the flow of energy related to pleasure and relationships.
3. **M - Solar Plexus Chakra (Manipura):**
   - The "M" sound corresponds to the Manipura or Solar Plexus Chakra, located in the upper abdomen.
   - Activation of the Solar Plexus Chakra is believed to enhance personal power, confidence, and the transformative energy related to digestion and metabolism.

4. **Silence (Turiya) - Heart Chakra (Anahata):**

   - The silence that follows the chanting of Aum, representing the transcendent or Turiya state, is often associated with the Heart Chakra.

   - Activation of the Heart Chakra is linked to love, compassion, and a sense of interconnectedness.

5. **Beyond Chakras - Throat, Third Eye, and Crown:**

   - The entire Aum sound, including the silence that follows, is considered to resonate with the Throat Chakra (Vishuddha), Third Eye Chakra (Ajna), and Crown Chakra (Sahasrara).

   - These higher chakras are associated with communication, intuition, spiritual insight, and the connection to higher consciousness.

When we are mindful of our breathing — aware of each breath, each instruction we send back to our body — we can consciously guide what manifests within us. By practicing proper, mindful breathing with the right balance of inhalation, exhalation, and retention, we can activate and manage our chakras, aligning the body in harmony. With every deep inhalation, we activate the chakras from top to bottom, filling them with pranvayu (life force). When our breath reaches the root chakra (Mooladhara), it energizes our whole being. Upon exhalation, we release impurities (vishuddhi) from the body, resonating with each chakra from the base to the crown, cleansing and balancing the body. Retention, in turn, allows the body to process the energy, preparing any remaining toxins to be expelled.

Proper breathing frees the brain from the constant noise of the mind. Otherwise, the mind pulls the brain into a cycle of overthinking, anxiety, and stress, continuously assessing the past or projecting onto the future. In doing so, the brain is pulled away from managing our present state, focusing instead on imagined threats. When the brain becomes busy with the mind's worries, it directs the body to react as though a threat were imminent, releasing stress chemicals and adjusting our breath accordingly. Meanwhile, the body's resources become depleted, leading to disorders — both mental and physical — because the energy needed to sustain it is diverted. Chronic stress convinces the brain that we are constantly in danger, using up vital resources that the body needs for well-being.

When we breathe properly, focusing mindfully on each breath, we allow the brain to return to its natural function — caring for the body. The brain is perfectly designed to manage this without conscious interference, but when we keep it preoccupied with the mind's distractions, it can't attend to the body's needs. This is why the breath maintains harmony between the mind, body, and brain.

Every thought, every word, is an affirmation — creating the reality that follows. Positive affirmations, whether spoken aloud or in your mind, shape your world. Allow yourself to feel whatever emotions arise, without judgment, but then take the time to affirm a more positive reality afterward. I encourage you to write down affirmations that serve as commands to your inner divine, and repeat them whenever you feel called to, especially in the morning or before sleep. Remember, affirmations aren't just what you say to yourself — they can also come from what others say to you, as long as you accept them.

Every thought reverberates in the Universal Mind, like a tuning fork, and this vibration influences the world around us. If sustained long enough, the vibration manifests as reality. In higher dimensions, this manifestation would happen instantly, but in our third-dimensional frequency, it takes time.

Our brain, based on our thoughts and the situation, decides which nadi to channel the pranvayu through — Ida, Pingala, or Sushumna. This activates either the sympathetic or parasympathetic system, preparing the body to respond to what it perceives as real. The brain doesn't know whether the situation is real or imagined — it reacts either way. This is why, when we are caught up in thoughts, stress, or anxiety, it is important to breathe properly and, if necessary, switch the flow of breath through the nadis to tell the brain that everything is okay. Mindful breathing — focusing on proper inhalation, exhalation, and retention — relaxes the brain, disconnecting it from the mind's stressful cycle of thoughts."

Ahamkara, Buddhi, Manas and Chitta

"Now" Bhog continued, "we will explore the Antahkarana, the four components of our mind. These are Ahamkara, Manas, Buddhi, and Chitta. They are the key players in shaping our consciousness and experiences."

Amara, sitting attentively at the front, asked, "Bhog, how do these four work together?"

Bhog smiled and began to explain. "Ahamkara, which we often call the ego, is the 'I-maker.' It is responsible for creating our sense of individuality. It's what makes us think in terms of 'I' and 'mine.' While it gives us a sense of identity, it can also create separation and attachment if we let it dominate our thoughts."

Amara, intrigued, leaned forward, "And how does Ahamkara influence the mind?"

Bhog nodded and continued, "Ahamkara shapes how we perceive ourselves and the world around us, influencing Manas, the thinking mind. Manas connects the external world through our senses and forms basic thoughts, emotions, and desires. It is always processing and reacting to stimuli — always busy, like a river constantly flowing."

Ravi, with his usual curiosity, asked, "How does Buddhi come into play?"

"Ah, Buddhi," Bhog said, "is the intellect, the faculty of discernment. While Manas reacts to the world, Buddhi evaluates and discerns. It helps us understand what is right and wrong, guiding our decisions. Buddhi can override the impulsive reactions of Manas, offering wisdom and clarity. It is the higher voice within us that seeks truth."

Kartik, reflecting on his own decision-making struggles, asked, "But what about Chitta, Bhog? How does it influence everything?"

"Chitta," Bhog explained, "is the storehouse of all our past experiences, memories, and subconscious impressions. It holds everything we've gone through, influencing our thoughts, emotions, and decisions without us even realizing it. Ahamkara, Manas, and Buddhi all draw from this reservoir of past experiences. It shapes how we act in the present, based on the imprints left from the past."

Aryan, the young boy who often felt torn between his emotions and thoughts, asked, "So, Bhog, how do we bring these four into harmony?"

Bhog smiled warmly. "It's about awareness, Aryan. Ahamkara, Manas, Buddhi, and Chitta are always interacting with each other. Ahamkara shapes your identity and influences Manas, which processes your desires and emotions. Buddhi helps guide these desires, offering wisdom, while Chitta continuously feeds past experiences into the mix. The key is to bring conscious awareness to this dynamic interplay. When Buddhi is strong, it can help you detach from the impulses of Ahamkara and the emotions of Manas, guiding you to act with wisdom rather than attachment."

Amara, always eager to deepen her understanding, asked, "How do we work with Chitta, Bhog, especially when it holds so many past impressions?"

"Through mindfulness, Amara," Bhog replied. "By becoming aware of the patterns stored in Chitta, we can bring these conditioned responses into the light of consciousness. Only then can we transform them. This practice requires us to look within and observe how our thoughts, emotions, and actions are shaped by our past. And, with time, we can release those patterns that no longer serve us."

The villagers nodded, absorbing the profound teachings. Bhog's words seemed to resonate deeply, offering them a glimpse into the intricate workings of their own minds.

"Remember," Bhog concluded, "these four — Ahamkara, Manas, Buddhi, and Chitta — are constantly at play. Through awareness and mindfulness, you can harmonize them, allowing your higher self to guide your actions. When Ahamkara surrenders to the wisdom of Buddhi, when Manas is balanced by discernment, and when Chitta is purified through awareness, you can live in a state of inner harmony."

With that, the villagers felt a renewed sense of understanding. They left the banyan tree with a deeper awareness of their inner workings, ready to apply Bhog's teachings in their everyday lives.

Power of Affirmations

Bhog sat under the shade of the banyan tree, his calm gaze sweeping over the gathered villagers. The morning was peaceful, but Bhog knew that within each heart, there were struggles — internal battles with ego, competition, and fear. He began to speak softly, yet his words carried the weight of deep wisdom.

"All diseases, my dear ones," Bhog began, "are born from the attachment to the ego, the self. It is our constant habit of attaching ourselves to outcomes, seeking validation through what we achieve or don't achieve, that causes so much suffering. The ego — the false sense of 'I' — creates this illusion. But if we can let go of this ego, if we can accept ourselves exactly as we are, without the need for competition, fear, or jealousy, we can free ourselves from suffering."

Amara, always striving to prove herself, listened closely, her heart resonating with the words. Bhog continued, "Imagine a life without the weight of guilt, anger, unsatisfaction, or greed. What if you simply accepted that who you are, right here, right now, is the best you can be? You were meant to be this way. There is nothing you need to change or achieve to be worthy. What you are today is enough."

Amara, who often felt the pressure to be more, to do more, felt a softening in her chest. "When we stop fighting with ourselves," Bhog said, "when we stop comparing, fearing, or striving for more, we open ourselves to the true beauty of life. In this moment, there is nothing more you need — no amount of money, food, or sex can give you the happiness that simply being alive, in this body, in this world, can offer."

The villagers were silent, taking in the gravity of Bhog's words. He then spoke about the essence of gratitude. "Thank the divine for what you have — the gift of being human in this beautiful world. Let go of fear, guilt, and jealousy, for they only hold you back. You are one of billions of people, all given the chance to live and experience the wonders of this life. And in that realization, there is freedom."

Ravi, who often felt the weight of his own expectations, asked, "But Bhog, how do we begin to let go of this attachment, this ego?"

Bhog smiled gently, "It begins with mindfulness, my child. It begins with experiencing life fully. Every bite of food you eat — tastes as though it were the first time. When you look at something, observe it with the eyes of wonder. When you touch, smell, or hear, experience it with your whole being. By doing this, we step out of our false identities, our egos, and connect with the real essence of life."

He paused for a moment, allowing his words to settle. Then, with compassion in his voice, he added, "Take some time to reflect on your life. Write down everything that has caused you pain — every wrong, every hurt. Write down the names of all who you believe have wronged you, even if that includes yourself. And then, forgive them. Forgive every single one, not for their sake, but for yours. This forgiveness is a gift to yourself, a way to free your body and mind from suffering. It is your way of telling your mind that it no longer needs to hold onto that pain."

Kartik, who had carried old grievances for years, felt a stirring in his heart. Bhog's next words were gentle but firm. "You see, forgiveness is not about letting others off the hook — it is about freeing yourself. The law of karma will take care of all actions, so you do not need to worry about justice. Everyone will meet the consequences of their actions. But you, you must be content with your own mind and body. Do not let any person, situation, or feeling take you off the path of mindfulness."

As the villagers absorbed Bhog's wisdom, they felt a sense of peace settling over them. Bhog's words offered them a way out of the cycles of anger, jealousy, and pain — a way to live in the present, free from the burdens of the past and the anxieties of the future.

"All you need to do," Bhog concluded, "is practice mindfulness. Be present. Accept yourself and others as they are. And let go of anything that keeps you from experiencing the bliss of this moment."

"Let me share with you a story about Sri Yukteshawar Giri Ji Maharaj. Many years ago, Sri Yukteswar shared with Paramhansa Yogananda an incident from his past when he sought healing from Lahiri Mahasaya in Benares. At the time, Yukteswar was recovering from a severe illness and was eager to gain weight. However, Lahiri Mahasaya's response was unexpected. Instead of acknowledging the physical aspect of Yukteswar's condition, he pointed out that Yukteswar had made himself unwell through his thoughts.

Lahiri Mahasaya's encouragement and a subtle form of healing led to an immediate improvement in Yukteswar's strength. Overjoyed, Yukteswar attributed the change to his guru's intervention. However, Lahiri Mahasaya insisted that it was Yukteswar's own thoughts that had alternately weakened and strengthened him.

Intrigued by this revelation, Yukteswar inquired whether he could regain his former weight simply by believing he was well. Lahiri Mahasaya affirmed that it was possible and, as he focused on Yukteswar's eyes, the disciple indeed felt an increase in both strength and weight. This transformation was not only instantaneous but also permanent.

Yukteswar returned to his mother's home, where his sudden physical change astonished friends and acquaintances. In just one day, he had gained fifty pounds, leading some individuals to become disciples of Lahiri Mahasaya due to the apparent miracle.

Sri Yukteswar concluded the story by explaining that the fully self-realized master, like Lahiri Mahasaya, understands the subtler laws governing the realms of consciousness and can influence the cosmic vision. These spiritual principles, beyond the scope of physical science, demonstrate the interconnectedness of mind and matter. The narrative also draws a parallel to Christ's ability to restore a severed ear, highlighting the universal nature of such miraculous acts across various spiritual traditions. Overall, the story serves as a reflection on the power of the mind, the spiritual dimensions of reality, and the profound influence of self-realized masters."

"In the teachings of our ancient scriptures," Bhog continued, "we learn about the profound connection between the mind, body, and spirit. Our thoughts, whether positive or negative, have the power to shape our lives, influence our health, and determine our happiness."

He glanced at the villagers, their eyes filled with curiosity, and continued, "Take, for instance, the **Yoga Sutras of Patanjali**. In Sutra 2.16, it is said that 'pain that has not yet come is avoidable.' This tells us that through mastery over the mind, we can prevent suffering before it manifests. Our thoughts can either lead us toward health or drag us toward pain."

Amara, always eager to understand deeper truths, asked, "Bhog, how do our thoughts impact our physical health?"

Bhog smiled gently. "The **Bhagavad Gita** speaks directly to this. In Chapter 6, Krishna tells Arjuna that the mind can be both our friend and our enemy. When we elevate our minds, filling them with positive, harmonious thoughts, we uplift ourselves. But when we allow negative thoughts — fear, anger, jealousy — to dominate, we degrade our own being."

He looked toward Ravi, who often struggled with self-doubt. "Our scriptures, like the **Ayurveda texts**, remind us that the mind and body are inseparable. Positive thoughts lead to a balanced, healthy life. Conversely, negative thoughts, attachments, and ego-driven desires weaken us, leading to illness. This is why Ayurveda places such importance on mental attitudes in healing."

Bhog paused for a moment, letting the words settle in, before speaking again. "In **Tantra** and **Yoga**, we learn about the energy centers in our bodies — the chakras. When our thoughts and emotions are in harmony, these chakras remain balanced, supporting our physical and mental well-being. Practices like meditation, affirmations, and mindfulness are tools to guide the mind and body toward healing."

Amara, who had experienced stress recently, asked, "Bhog, are there modern examples that align with what our scriptures teach?"

Bhog nodded. "There are indeed. Many people today, like **Dr. Joe Dispenza** and **Louise Hay**, have shared their stories of self-healing through the power of the mind. Dr. Dispenza used visualization and meditation to heal himself from a severe spinal injury. He believed in the mind's capacity to trigger the body's healing mechanisms, much like our ancient teachings suggest."

He added, "Louise Hay, too, overcame cancer by practicing positive affirmations. She believed that our thoughts and emotions are directly linked to physical conditions, and by transforming those thoughts, we can heal ourselves. Both of these modern stories echo the wisdom found in our **Upanishads**, where the mind is seen as the creator of our reality."

Ravi leaned forward, fascinated. "So, Bhog, our minds can either make us sick or help us heal?"

Bhog's eyes twinkled. "Exactly, Ravi. Our subconscious mind accepts every command we send, whether positive or negative. If we constantly feed it thoughts of fear, guilt, and anger, it will manifest those in our physical bodies. But if we fill our minds with love, gratitude, and peace, we cultivate health and happiness."

Bhog's voice softened as he continued, "In our day-to-day lives, we often forget how powerful our thoughts truly are. Every word, every thought we have is like an affirmation, a command to the universe, and the universe responds in kind. When we embrace positive affirmations, like Dr. Dispenza or Louise Hay did, we set in motion the process of self-healing."

He encouraged the villagers to take a moment for introspection. "Write down the negative thoughts and emotions that have weighed you down. Write down the names of those who have hurt you, and forgive them — not for their sake, but for your own. This act of forgiveness, of letting go, will free you from the burden of negativity. It tells your body and mind that you no longer need to carry that pain."

Amara asked, "How can we start practicing this, Bhog?"

Bhog replied, "Start with small, simple affirmations. Speak words of kindness to yourself — 'I am healthy, I am happy, I am enough.' Recite them throughout your day, and let your mind begin to accept this new reality. The more you engage in these affirmations, the more you'll begin to see changes in your life."

With those words, Bhog left the villagers with a newfound understanding of their own power. The teachings of the scriptures and modern examples like Dr. Dispenza and Louise Hay had shown them that true healing begins within. They now knew that by mastering their minds, they could shape their lives, their health, and their happiness.

A Yogic and Sattvic lifestyle

Next morning, as the sun rose over the village, Bhog sat under the ancient banyan tree, preparing to guide the gathered villagers toward living a Yogic and Sattvic lifestyle. The air was fresh, the atmosphere peaceful, and the people were eager to hear Bhog's wisdom. Bhog had a calm yet focused demeanor as he began to speak about how they could integrate these principles into their daily lives, blending the teachings of ancient texts with practical, holistic approaches to well-being.

1. Yogic Practices: The Foundation of Harmony

Bhog started with the importance of **Yogic practices** in creating a balanced, harmonious life. “Dear ones,” Bhog said gently, “the body is a temple, and our physical well-being is tied to our spiritual growth. By practicing asanas (physical postures), pranayama (breath control), and meditation daily, we maintain the temple, keep it pure, and allow the mind and spirit to flourish.”

Amara, who had recently been feeling restless, asked, “But Bhog, how can we incorporate these practices in our busy lives?”

Bhog smiled and responded, “Start small. Begin with a few minutes of pranayama each morning. I suggest following the **4-2-4-2** breathing technique — inhaling for four seconds, holding the breath for two seconds, exhaling for four seconds, and holding again for two seconds. Over time, this pattern becomes natural. It not only calms the mind but also harmonizes your chakras, filling your body with the **Pran Vayu** it needs.”

He emphasized that this practice could:

1. Keep the mind centered and mindful.
2. Ensure the body receives enough prana to energize each organ.
3. Create a lasting sense of peace and bliss.

Amara, who had been struggling with stress, nodded, sensing that this simple practice could bring balance to her life.

2. **The Sattvic Diet: Nourishment for the Soul**

   Bhog then moved on to the importance of food, explaining the concept of a **Sattvic diet**, which focuses on foods that are pure, nourishing, and harmonious. "Food is not just for the body; it is for the soul," Bhog said, "A Sattvic diet consists of fresh fruits, vegetables, whole grains, nuts, seeds, and dairy. But remember, dairy should only be consumed if it comes from a source where animals are loved and cared for."

   Kartik, who often found himself eating processed food out of convenience, asked, "Bhog, how can I adopt a Sattvic diet with all the temptations around me?"

   Bhog replied thoughtfully, "Begin by incorporating small changes. Replace one processed meal with fresh vegetables or fruits. Gradually, your body will crave the purity of Sattvic foods. And when you eat, do so mindfully — savor each bite, express gratitude, and avoid overeating."

3. **Intermittent Fasting: The Power of Autophagy**

   Bhog then explained the benefits of **intermittent fasting** and how it aligns with the body's natural rhythm, stimulating **autophagy**, a process where the body cleanses and repairs itself at a cellular level.

   Aryan, always curious, asked, "Bhog, what is this autophagy, and why is it important?"

   Bhog smiled and answered, "Autophagy is the body's way of removing old, damaged cells and making space for new, healthy ones. By fasting periodically, you allow your body to heal itself, improving your physical and mental health."

4. Mindful Eating: Savoring Every Moment

As Bhog spoke of **mindful eating**, he encouraged the villagers to experience their food fully. "When you eat," he said, "do so with awareness. Taste each flavor, feel the texture, and be present in the moment."

Amara, who often rushed through her meals, asked, "But how can we slowdown in our busy lives?"

"Start by focusing on one meal a day," Bhog suggested. "Sit quietly, free of distractions, and enjoy each bite. This will transform how you feel about eating, making it a meditative practice."

5. Selfless Service: Seva as a Path to Peace

"Selfless service, or **Seva**," Bhog continued, "is an essential aspect of a Sattvic lifestyle. By helping others without expecting anything in return, you cultivate humility and compassion."

Ravi, who often felt disconnected from his community, asked, "How can I practice Seva?"

Bhog responded, "Begin by helping someone in need. It could be as simple as assisting an elderly person with their chores, sharing food with those who are hungry, or simply offering kind words. Each act of selflessness brings you closer to the divine."

6. Nature Connection: Reconnecting with the Earth

Bhog urged the villagers to spend more time in nature. "By walking among the trees, feeling the wind on your face, and listening to the sounds of birds, you align yourself with the natural rhythms of the Earth."

Kartik, who rarely found time for such activities, asked, "How do we make time for this?"

"Even a short walk in nature each day can help," Bhog replied. "Connect with the earth, and you will find a deeper sense of peace."

7. **Self-Affirmations: Reprogramming the Mind**

   Finally, Bhog spoke about the power of **self-affirmations** in healing. "The mind," he said, "accepts whatever instructions you give it. If you constantly feed it negative thoughts, it will create a reality based on those thoughts. But if you practice positive affirmations, you begin to reprogram your mind."

   He encouraged the villagers to create personalized affirmations like:

   - "I am healthy, peaceful, and full of life."
   - "I attract love, joy, and abundance into my life."

   Bhog suggested writing down these affirmations and repeating them daily, either in the morning or before sleep. "This practice," he said, "creates a ripple effect in the mind and body, aligning your reality with your intentions."

8. **Moderation and Spiritual Growth**

   Bhog emphasized the need for **moderation in sensory experiences**, advising the villagers to avoid excessive noise, screen time, or overstimulation. "Balance," he said, "is key to inner peace."

He encouraged regular **self-reflection** and the exploration of sacred texts. "By understanding the teachings of our scriptures and reflecting on them, you nurture your spirit and deepen your connection with the divine."

Amara, who had been deeply affected by stress and anxiety, took Bhog's teachings to heart. She began practicing the 4-2-4-2 breathing technique every morning, adopted a Sattvic diet, and introduced self-affirmations into her daily routine. Slowly, she noticed a shift. The restlessness in her mind began to ease, and she felt a deep sense of contentment she hadn't known before.

One day, she approached Bhog under the banyan tree. "Bhog," she said, "I feel lighter, more at peace. Your teachings have helped me find balance in my life."

Bhog smiled warmly. "The answers were always within you, Amara. You simply needed to reconnect with your true self. Continue on this path, and the peace you feel now will only deepen."

By the time Bhog finished, the villagers were filled with a newfound sense of purpose. They had learned that living a Yogic and Sattvic lifestyle wasn't about drastic changes, but about integrating small, mindful practices into their daily lives — practices that nurtured the body, mind, and spirit.

In the quiet village where the gentle hum of daily life resonated, Bhog stood as a beacon of wisdom, a living repository of knowledge that transcended the boundaries of time. As the sun dipped below the horizon, casting a warm glow over the cobblestone streets, the villages folk gathered around Bhog, eager to absorb the final fragments of his teachings.

Bhog, with his weathered face and eyes that sparkled with the light of countless experiences, began weaving the concluding threads of his discourse. His words, like ethereal notes, danced through the air, carrying the essence of profound insights and timeless truths.

"My dear friends," Bhog began, "as we stand at the threshold of another day, let us not forget the lessons we've shared. Life, like a grand tapestry, is woven with the threads of joy and sorrow, success and failure, laughter and tears. Embrace it all, for each moment contributes to the masterpiece of your existence."

The village people listened intently, their hearts resonating with the simplicity and depth of Bhog's teachings. He continued, "In the tapestry of life, remember that every encounter, every challenge, is a teacher. Learn from the melodies of joy and let the dissonance of sorrow sculpt your resilience. For within the symphony of opposites lies the harmony of your being."

As Bhog spoke, the stars emerged, casting their soft glow upon the gathering. He imparted the wisdom of interconnectedness, emphasizing the threads that bind every soul in the cosmic fabric of existence. "See the divinity in each other, for in recognizing the sacredness of every being, you open the door to compassion and unity."

The village, once a mere backdrop to mundane routines, now echoed with the profound teachings of Bhog. His words were not just lessons but invitations to awaken the dormant seeds of self-realization within each listener.

Chapter 4

Ideology

Dharma Artha Kama Moksha

Bhog sat in quiet contemplation under the shade of the banyan tree as the villagers gathered around him. A man in the front row, his face showing a mix of curiosity and concern, raised his hand and asked, "Bhog, what is Dharma, Artha, Kama, and Moksha? And what are my responsibilities as a normal human being living a household life?"

With a serene smile, Bhog nodded and began to speak, his words calm yet profound, "The four goals of life, known as Purusharthas — Dharma, Artha, Kama, and Moksha — are the pillars upon which our existence is built. These guide us on how to live a balanced, fulfilling, and righteous life."

Dharma (Righteousness and Duty)

"Dharma," Bhog said, "is the foundation. It refers to the ethical and moral principles that govern our lives. Dharma is about performing your duties with integrity, honesty, and a sense of responsibility — not just towards yourself but towards society and the universe. As a householder, your dharma includes fulfilling obligations to your family, your work, your community, and the world at large."

Bhog paused and then continued, "Imagine you are a thread in a vast web, and your actions, words, and thoughts affect every other thread in that web. That is Dharma — living in harmony with the world around you, ensuring that your actions contribute to the greater good."

He then gave an example of a farmer in the village, who tirelessly worked to cultivate the land not just for his family but for the benefit of the entire community. “His work is dharma. It is a selfless action that upholds the well-being of others while fulfilling his personal responsibilities.”

Bhog explained further, “Dharma for a householder means supporting your family, being truthful, helping others in need, respecting elders, and protecting the environment. It also involves following the laws of the land and maintaining harmony with society. However, dharma also extends to yourself — taking care of your body and mind, living a disciplined life, and practicing self-restraint.”

“Dharma,” Bhog emphasized, “is the guiding force that helps us maintain balance between personal desires and the needs of others. It ensures that our actions are not driven by selfish motives but by a higher sense of purpose.”

Artha (Material Prosperity)

Bhog then shifted his focus to Artha, the pursuit of material prosperity. “Artha is essential because it provides us with the resources, we need to live a comfortable life and to support our family and society. Wealth in itself is not evil, but the pursuit of wealth must be aligned with Dharma.”

He looked at the crowd and said, “Think of Artha as the fuel for your responsibilities. A householder has to earn wealth to take care of their family, to educate their children, and to contribute to society. But remember, the way you earn wealth must be righteous — never through deceit, exploitation, or harming others.”

Bhog continued, “In the life of a Karma Yogi, wealth is seen not as an end but as a means to serve a higher purpose. A Karma Yogi works hard, earning wealth through honest and ethical means, but remains detached from it. Wealth should flow like water, nourishing the fields of duty and service but never stagnating or becoming the sole focus of life."

He then gave the example of a successful merchant in the village, who not only provided for his family but also used his wealth to help build schools and support community events. "That," Bhog said, "is the true purpose of Artha. It should benefit not just you, but also others. A Karma Yogi recognizes that prosperity is a gift, one that should be shared with the world."

Bhog paused for a moment, allowing the villagers to reflect on their own relationship with wealth. He added, "At the same time, you must be mindful of not becoming attached to wealth. The pursuit of material prosperity should not lead you away from Dharma, and it should never become the sole measure of your success."

Kama (Desire and Pleasure)

Bhog then moved on to Kama, the pursuit of desires and pleasures. "Kama refers to all the desires that bring us joy — whether through love, art, music, or the enjoyment of life's pleasures. These desires are not inherently wrong. In fact, they are part of the human experience."

He looked around at the villagers and continued, "But Kama must always be guided by Dharma. Desires and pleasures should be pursued in a way that doesn't harm others or lead you away from your duties. A Karma Yogi enjoys life's pleasures but with moderation and mindfulness. They don't become slaves to their desires."

Bhog then shared a story about a young man in the village who became obsessed with wealth and pleasure, neglecting his duties and responsibilities. "At first, he found joy in the material world, but soon he felt empty, disconnected from his family and his own soul. He realized that without Dharma, the pursuit of Kama led only to suffering."

He emphasized that it is natural to seek happiness in relationships, beauty, and experiences, but when desires are unchecked, they lead to attachment, which can cause suffering. "A Karma Yogi enjoys the beauty of life but remains unattached, knowing that true happiness comes from within, not from external objects."

Bhog reminded the villagers that love, relationships, and pleasures are divine gifts, but they must be experienced with awareness and a sense of balance. "When you enjoy life's pleasures without becoming overly attached, you maintain inner peace. That is the path of a Karma Yogi in Kama."

Moksha (Spiritual Liberation)

Bhog's voice softened as he spoke about Moksha, the ultimate goal of life. "Moksha is liberation from the cycle of birth and death, the realization of your true self, and the attainment of spiritual freedom. It is the understanding that you are not this body or mind but something far greater — a spark of the divine."

"Moksha," Bhog continued, "is the ultimate goal of every soul. While you live in this world, fulfilling your duties, earning wealth, and enjoying pleasures, your actions should always be oriented towards spiritual growth. A Karma Yogi seeks Moksha not by renouncing the world but by living in it, performing duties with selflessness and detachment."

He explained that Moksha is not something to be achieved only after death. "It is a state of being that can be experienced in this lifetime. When you act without attachment, when you surrender the fruits of your actions to the divine, and when you realize that you are part of something much greater, you are walking the path to Moksha."

Bhog shared a story of an old woman in the village who spent her life caring for others, never seeking praise or recognition. "She lived simply, performing her duties with love and devotion. In her later years, she realized the peace of Moksha, not by abandoning her responsibilities, but by fulfilling them with detachment."

Integrating Dharma, Artha, Kama, and Moksha

Bhog then looked at the man who had asked the question and said, "These four pursuits — Dharma, Artha, Kama, and Moksha — are not separate. They are intertwined, guiding you towards a balanced life."

"As a householder," Bhog explained, "you fulfill your Dharma by taking care of your family and society. You pursue Artha to provide for your material needs. You enjoy Kama, experiencing the beauty and joy of life. And through all of this, you work towards Moksha by living a life of selflessness, detachment, and awareness."

Bhog continued, "The key is balance. Too much focus on one and you lose sight of the others. Pursue Artha and Kama, but let them be guided by Dharma, and always keep your heart open to the ultimate goal of Moksha."

Bhog shared a story to further explain the balance of these pursuits.

There was once a wealthy merchant who lived in a village similar to ours. He had accumulated vast wealth through honest means, but despite his riches, he felt a void in his heart. He traveled to seek the advice of a wise sage.

The sage, seeing the merchant's troubled expression, asked, "What burdens you, my friend?"

The merchant replied, "I have earned wealth and enjoyed life's pleasures, but I feel something is missing. I have wealth, yet I do not feel fulfilled."

The sage smiled and said, "You have pursued Artha and Kama well, but have you considered Dharma and Moksha? Wealth and pleasure alone will not bring lasting fulfillment."

The merchant thought for a moment and asked, "But how do I balance them?"

The sage replied, "Serve others with your wealth, enjoy life's pleasures with moderation, fulfill your duties with love, and seek the divine in all that you do. In doing so, you will find peace."

The merchant took the sage's advice to heart, and in time, he found the fulfillment he had been seeking, not in his wealth or pleasures, but in living a balanced life of service, duty, and devotion.

Bhog then gave practical advice for the villagers to integrate these teachings into their daily lives:

- **For Dharma:** Start each day by reflecting on your responsibilities. Ask yourself, "How can I contribute to the well-being of my family, society, and the world today?" Practice kindness, honesty, and integrity in all that you do.
- **For Artha:** Work hard, but always with a sense of purpose. Use your wealth to help others, whether by supporting a family member, contributing to a community project, or simply being generous. Never let wealth become your master.
- **For Kama:** Enjoy the pleasures of life — whether it's through relationships, art, or nature — but do so mindfully. Let your

enjoyment be in balance with your responsibilities and never let desires consume you.

- **For Moksha:** Set aside time each day for meditation and self-reflection. Practice detachment by letting go of the results of your actions. Know that true liberation comes not from renouncing the world but from living in it with awareness and selflessness.

As Bhog finished, he looked around at the villagers and said, "Life is a delicate dance between these four pursuits. When you live in alignment with Dharma, seek Artha with righteousness, enjoy Kama with moderation, and strive for Moksha with detachment, you will find both worldly fulfillment and spiritual peace."

The villagers, filled with clarity and purpose, bowed to Bhog in gratitude, ready to embrace the teachings and apply them in their daily lives. As they left, Bhog's final words echoed in their hearts, "Live with balance, live with awareness, and you will find true fulfillment."

Four Purusharthas

Ravi in the front row raised his hand and asked, "Bhog, can you explain the four ashrams — the stages of life — and how they connect with the four purusharthas or goals of life? What are our responsibilities as we move through each stage of life?"

Bhog, his face serene and calm, nodded. "Ah, the ashrams and purusharthas — the stages and goals of life. These are the pillars of Hindu philosophy, guiding us from birth to liberation. Each stage of life, or ashram, aligns with specific duties (dharma) and goals (purusharthas), helping us grow both materially and spiritually. Let us begin with the first stage."

Brahmacharya (Student Stage)

Bhog's voice carried through the quiet of the village, "The first stage of life is Brahmacharya, the student stage. In this stage, your primary focus is on learning and education. As a student, your dharma is to dedicate yourself to acquiring knowledge, not just academic but also moral and spiritual. The teacher, or Guru, becomes central in your life, and through their guidance, you learn the disciplines of Jnana Yoga — the yoga of knowledge. The dharma here is to lay the foundation of a righteous life."

Yash sitting nearby listened intently. Bhog smiled at him and continued, "In Brahmacharya, you also lay the groundwork for Artha, which is the responsible pursuit of material well-being later in life. The knowledge you gain here will help you earn a living, contribute to society, and support your future family."

He paused, allowing the crowd to absorb his words before continuing, "But remember, this stage isn't just about preparing for wealth. The true artha here is acquiring the skills and values that will guide you through life. It's about learning self-discipline, honesty, and integrity."

Grihastha (Householder Stage)

Bhog then moved to the next stage, the one most villager were living in. "The second stage, Grihastha, is the householder stage. This is where most of you are right now. In this stage, dharma shifts to fulfilling your responsibilities to your family, to society, and to yourself. You become a provider, a spouse, and a parent. You contribute to society through your work and through raising your children with the same values of dharma you learned in your youth."

Bhog noticed several parents in the crowd nodding, recognizing their roles in this stage. "As a householder," he continued, "the pursuit of Artha becomes central. But Artha here is not just about acquiring wealth; it's about doing so ethically. You must ensure that the wealth you accumulate is through righteous means, that it supports your family and community, and that it doesn't become a source of greed or corruption."

Bhog's gaze shifted to a young couple in the crowd. "Then comes Kama, the fulfillment of desires. In the householder stage, you experience love, relationships, and the pleasures of life. But these desires must always be guided by dharma. You enjoy life's pleasures — be it through your family, your work, or your community — but never at the expense of your responsibilities. The enjoyment of pleasure must be balanced with duty."

He paused, allowing the young couple to reflect on their roles before speaking again. "This stage is also where spiritual growth begins. Though you are immersed in worldly duties, you must not forget the goal of Moksha, the liberation of the soul. Even in your busy life, set aside time for prayer, meditation, and acts of selflessness. Through this balance of Dharma, Artha, Kama, and the pursuit of Moksha, you walk the path of a Karma Yogi — one who seeks liberation through action."

Vanaprastha (Retirement Stage)

Bhog then moved to the third stage, the Vanaprastha, or retirement stage. "After fulfilling your duties as a householder, you gradually withdraw from worldly responsibilities. This is the time of Vanaprastha, the stage of contemplation and spiritual focus. You pass on your knowledge to the next generation, guide them in their paths, but your focus now shifts towards deepening your spiritual practice."

Several elders in the crowd listened closely as Bhog continued, "In this stage, the pursuit of Artha lessens. You begin to detach from material wealth and possessions. The focus shifts toward spiritual Artha — accumulating wisdom and understanding the deeper truths of life."

Bhog glanced at the older men and women, their faces softened by years of experience. "Desires, or Kama, also begin to reduce in this stage. Your joy comes from simplicity, from spiritual practices, and from the peace that arises from within. You are preparing your soul for the final stage, that of renunciation."

"The main goal of this stage," Bhog continued, "is to prepare for Moksha. You spend more time in meditation, in nature, and in the study of scriptures. You're not yet renouncing the world, but you are beginning the process of letting go. It is a time of spiritual reflection and readiness for the final liberation."

Sannyasa (Renunciant Stage)

Finally, Bhog reached the fourth and last stage, Sannyasa. "In this final stage, you renounce all worldly attachments. You no longer belong to a family, to wealth, or to society. You belong only to the divine. The primary duty here is to seek Moksha — spiritual liberation from the cycle of birth and death. You dedicate yourself entirely to meditation, self-realization, and service to the world, but without any attachment."

The villagers were silent, contemplating the gravity of renunciation. Bhog's voice was soft yet powerful as he continued, "In Sannyasa, Artha has no place. You give up material possessions and attachments. Even Kama, the desires that once fueled your householder life, have faded away. Your sole focus is on Moksha — union with the divine. You become free from the bonds of this world."

Bhog shared a story about a renowned saint who, after living a life of responsibility and duty, renounced everything and spent his days in deep meditation and selfless service. "He realized that true freedom lies not in what you possess or achieve, but in what you can let go of. Sannyasa is the ultimate letting go."

Bhog then tied the four ashrams to the four purusharthas — the goals of life. "Each stage of life is aligned with a specific goal. In Brahmacharya, the focus is on Dharma — the learning and cultivation of ethics and knowledge. You prepare yourself for life's responsibilities. In Grihastha, the focus is on Artha and Kama — earning wealth and fulfilling desires, but always within the bounds of Dharma. In Vanaprastha, the goal shifts back towards Dharma and Moksha — preparing for spiritual liberation. And in Sannyasa, the sole focus is on Moksha — freedom from the cycle of birth and death."

Bhog added, "But remember, these stages and goals are not strictly linear. Even in the householder stage, you should always keep one eye on Moksha, just as in Sannyasa, you still uphold Dharma. The balance of these four purusharthas is what makes life harmonious."

Bhog then gave practical advice for applying these teachings in daily life:

- **Brahmacharya (Student Stage):** "For the youth among you, focus on your education and discipline. Learn not just from books, but from the world around you. Absorb the lessons of nature, of kindness, of ethics. This is the foundation of your life."

- **Grihastha (Householder Stage):** "For those of you in the householder stage, balance your duties with your desires. Provide for your family, but also give back to society. Enjoy life, but don't become attached to its pleasures. Always keep Moksha in mind, even amidst your responsibilities."

- **Vanaprastha (Retirement Stage):** "For those entering retirement, start withdrawing from material attachments. Spend more time in nature, with yourself, in contemplation. Guide the younger generation but focus on preparing your soul for liberation."
- **Sannyasa (Renunciant Stage):** "For those ready to renounce, let go of all attachments. Your only duty now is to the divine. Meditate, serve selflessly, and seek union with the higher consciousness."

Bhog concluded with a final thought, "The journey of life, through the four ashrams and guided by the four purusharthas, is one of balance, growth, and liberation. Each stage has its duties and its goals, but all are aimed at one ultimate truth — self-realization and freedom. Walk this path with awareness, with gratitude, and with love, and you will find the fulfillment that every soul seeks."

The villagers, filled with new understanding, bowed to Bhog in gratitude, ready to embrace the teachings in their lives. As they dispersed, Bhog's words lingered in the air, reminding them of the sacred journey they were all a part of.

Life Ideologies we can follow from Indian Scriptures

Ideology of Ashtavakra Gita

As the sun set behind the rolling hills, casting a golden hue across the village, the usual calm under the banyan tree was once again punctuated by the soft rustling of leaves. Bhog sat at the center, his presence as peaceful as the still air. The villagers had gathered, including familiar faces from our cast — Ravi, Amara, Arjun, Kartik, Anika, Yash, Radha, Kalpana, and Maya. Their faces reflected curiosity, anticipation, and a thirst for understanding life's deeper meanings.

Ravi, always the inquisitive one, raised his hand first. “Bhog, I’ve been thinking a lot about the Ashtavakra Gita. It’s so profound, but how do we apply its wisdom in our everyday lives?”

Bhog smiled warmly at Ravi. “Ah, my dear Ravi, the teachings of the Ashtavakra Gita may seem abstract, but they are meant to be lived, not just understood. Let’s explore how each of you can apply this wisdom as you walk the path of your daily lives.”

1. **Detachment from Material Possessions**

   Amara, with her artistic soul, leaned forward. “Bhog, I sometimes find myself too attached to the success of my creative work. How can I let go of this attachment?”

   Bhog’s eyes twinkled with understanding. “Amara, the Ashtavakra Gita teaches that material possessions, including the outcomes of your creativity, are fleeting. The key is to enjoy the process of creation without being attached to the result. Let your art flow through you as an expression of the divine, and once it is created, release it into the world without expectation. This will bring you peace, not only in your art but in every aspect of your life.”

   Amara nodded thoughtfully, already sensing how freeing that could be.

2. **Equanimity in Dualities**

   Ravi, restless in his teenage energy, asked, “How can we stay calm when life throws challenges at us? I feel frustrated when things don’t go my way.”

   Bhog turned his attention to Ravi. “The Ashtavakra Gita speaks of equanimity, my young friend. Life will always present dualities — pleasure and pain, success and failure.

The secret is not to resist these opposites but to embrace them with balance. Imagine standing in a storm, Ravi. If you sway too much to either side, you'll be knocked down. But if you stand firm, rooted in your center, the storm will pass, and you will remain steady. Practice mindfulness in each situation, and soon you'll find that inner calm, no matter what life brings."

Ravi smiled, feeling a new sense of determination.

3. **Recognition of the Impermanent Self**

Kartik, who often struggled with balancing his responsibilities, asked, "Bhog, I feel so tied to my roles as a father, husband, and provider. How do I manage this without losing myself?"

Bhog looked at Kartik with gentle empathy. "Kartik, the Ashtavakra Gita reminds us that our true self is beyond these roles. You are not just a father, husband, or provider; these are temporary identities that help you navigate the world. But within you, beyond these roles, lies your eternal self. The more you connect with that inner self-through moments of silence and self-reflection — the less you will feel burdened by the roles you play. Your responsibilities are important, but they do not define you."

Kartik let out a deep breath, as if a weight had been lifted.

4. **Action with Detached Involvement**

Arjun, wise with age but still active in his work, asked, "Bhog, how can I perform my duties without getting too caught up in the outcome? I've lived my whole life striving for success."

Bhog smiled at the elder. "Arjun, the Gita teaches us to perform our actions with full dedication but without attachment to the fruits. It is your duty to act, but the results are not in your hands. Just as a farmer plants the seeds and waters the soil, it is not the farmer who decides when and how much the crops will grow. Focus on your efforts and let go of the outcome. This is the essence of detached involvement."

Arjun nodded, the wisdom resonating with his life's experiences.

5. Self-Realization and Inner Silence

Anika, now in the later stages of her life, asked softly, "Bhog, how do I find inner silence amidst the noise of daily life? I long for peace, but it seems elusive."

Bhog's face softened with kindness. "Anika, inner silence is not found by escaping the world but by embracing it fully while staying connected to your center. Begin by setting aside a few minutes each day for quiet reflection. Sit with your breath, and simply observe without judgment. As you practice, this silence will grow within you, even in the midst of activity. The silence is not outside; it is within, always waiting for you."

Anika closed her eyes, as if already seeking that inner peace.

6. Compassion and Non-Judgment

Radha, nurturing and kind, spoke up next. "Bhog, sometimes I find it hard not to judge others, especially when I feel hurt. How can I be more compassionate?"

Bhog nodded, understanding the struggle. "Radha, the Ashtavakra Gita reminds us that everyone is on their own journey, shaped by their own experiences and limitations. When someone hurts you, it is often because they are hurt themselves. Compassion comes when you realize that we are all connected, all part of the same divine consciousness. Try to see the divine in others, even when they cannot see it in themselves. When you do this, judgment fades, and love takes its place."

Radha smiled, feeling a warm sense of connection to those around her.

7. **Simplicity and Contentment**

   Yash, young and full of dreams, asked, "Bhog, how do I find contentment when there's so much I want to achieve in life?"

   Bhog chuckled softly. "Ah, Yash, your ambition is natural, but remember, contentment does not come from achieving everything on your list. The Ashtavakra Gita teaches that true contentment arises from within. Simplify your desires. Focus on what truly matters — love, truth, and inner peace. Achieve, yes, but do not let your achievements define your happiness. Contentment is a state of being, not something you attain."

   Yash looked thoughtful, contemplating how he could shift his perspective.

8. **Service and Generosity**

   Kalpana, the youngest in the group, asked with her innocent curiosity, "Bhog, how can I help others when I'm so small?"

Bhog's heart warmed at her question. "Kalpana, you may be small, but your heart is vast. You can help others through small acts of kindness — sharing your toys, offering a smile, listening when someone needs to talk. Service is not about grand gestures; it's about the love behind the action. Every little bit counts, and your kindness will ripple out into the world."

Kalpana beamed; her smile as bright as the sun setting behind the tree.

As the evening wore on, Bhog gathered the group with his final thoughts. "The Ashtavakra GIta offers us wisdom that is timeless, and each of you, in your own way, can live by these principles. Detach from material desires, embrace equanimity, act with love but without attachment, and seek the silence within. Life, with all its responsibilities and challenges, is your spiritual path. Walk it with awareness, love, and gratitude."

Ideology of Bhagavad Gita

Ravi, filled with youthful curiosity, broke the silence, "Bhog, we often hear about the Bhagavad Gita and its wisdom. How can we apply its teachings in our daily lives?"

Bhog's eyes sparkled as he smiled at the group. "Ah, the Bhagavad Gita, a scripture that holds the essence of life. It is not just a guide for warriors like Arjuna, but for all of us who face battles within. Let's explore how you, as householders, students, and seekers, can live the teachings of Krishna."

1. **Dharma and Duty**

   Kartik, feeling the weight of his responsibilities as a father and provider, asked, "Bhog, how can I fulfill my duties without feeling overwhelmed?"

   Bhog responded gently, "Kartik, Krishna teaches us about Dharma — our duty. It is not the weight of responsibility that overwhelms us, but the attachment to outcomes. Perform your duties with love but let go of the need for control. Whether as a father, a husband, or a provider, know that you are fulfilling your Dharma. That is enough."

Kartik nodded, feeling a sense of relief wash over him.

2. **Detachment and Selfless Action**

   Amara, who often felt frustrated when her creative projects didn't yield the success she hoped for, asked, "How can I continue my work without being attached to the results?"

   Bhog smiled warmly, "Amara, Krishna teaches Karma Yoga — the path of selfless action. Create with all your heart, but do not attach your happiness to the outcome. The joy lies in the act of creation itself, not in the applause it may or may not receive. When you let go of the need for validation, you will find true fulfillment."

   Amara's heart lightened as she reflected on how freeing that approach could be.

3. **Equanimity in Joy and Sorrow**

   Ravi, with his boundless energy, asked, "Bhog, I get really upset when things don't go my way. How can I stay calm when life gets tough?"

   Bhog leaned forward and said, "Ravi, the Gita teaches us about equanimity — seeing joy and sorrow as two sides of the same coin. Life will always have its ups and downs. It's how you respond that matters. Train your mind to be steady, like a candle flame in the wind. When you cultivate balance, you will not be shaken by life's storms."

   Ravi smiled, already feeling a sense of peace from Bhog's words.

4. **Yoga and Union**

Anika, spiritually inclined and seeking deeper understanding, asked, "Bhog, which path of yoga should I follow to connect with the divine?"

Bhog looked at her with compassion. "Anika, Krishna speaks of different paths — Bhakti Yoga for devotion, Karma Yoga for selfless action, Jnana Yoga for knowledge, and Raja Yoga for meditation. Follow the path that resonates with your heart. You can practice devotion through love, knowledge through study, and meditation through silence. Ultimately, they all lead to union with the divine."

Anika closed her eyes, feeling connected to her spiritual journey.

5. **Compassion and Non-Violence**

Radha, nurturing and kind, asked, "Bhog, how can we practice compassion even when others hurt us?"

Bhog's gaze softened. "Radha, Krishna teaches us to act without malice and to see the divine in all beings. When someone causes you pain, understand that they are acting from their own suffering. Respond with compassion, not anger. This doesn't mean allowing harm but approaching each situation with empathy. Compassion heals both the giver and the receiver."

Radha felt a warm glow of understanding spread through her heart.

6. **Discipline and Self-Control**

Yash, still figuring out his place in the world, asked, "How do I develop discipline in my life, Bhog?"

Bhog chuckled, "Ah, young Yash, Krishna speaks of the importance of Tapas — discipline and self-control. It's not about being rigid but about creating healthy habits that support your growth. Start small — whether it's a daily meditation practice, mindful eating, or dedicating time to study. Over time, these small disciplines will build inner strength."

Yash nodded eagerly, ready to take the first steps toward discipline.

7. **Service to Others**

   Arjun, with his years of wisdom, asked, "How do we serve others without expecting anything in return?"

   Bhog looked at him with admiration. "Arjun, service is the highest form of devotion. Krishna speaks of Seva — selfless service — as a way to express love for the divine. When you help others, do so without seeking recognition or reward. The joy lies in the act of giving. The moment you expect something in return, the purity of the action is diminished."

   Arjun smiled, realizing that true service came from the heart.

8. **Surrender to the Divine Will**

   Anika, still pondering her spiritual path, asked, "Bhog, how do I surrender to the divine will when I feel lost?"

   Bhog's voice was soft but firm. "Anika, surrender is not about giving up — it's about letting go of the need to control. Krishna teaches that everything is part of the divine plan. Trust that there is a higher purpose guiding your life, even when the path seems unclear. Surrender your fears and trust the process. The divine will carry you."

Anika closed her eyes, feeling a deep sense of trust in the unknown.

9. Balance of Material and Spiritual Life

Kartik, once again feeling the weight of worldly responsibilities, asked, “Bhog, how do I balance my material responsibilities with my spiritual aspirations?”

Bhog smiled gently. “Kartik, the Bhagavad Gita teaches us to find balance between the material and the spiritual. You do not need to renounce the world to be spiritual. Fulfill your duties as a father and provider but make time for your spiritual practices as well. Meditate, reflect, and connect with the divine in your heart. The key is balance, not sacrifice.”

Kartik felt a sense of peace, knowing that he could walk both paths.

10. Overcoming Fear

Kalpana, the youngest and full of wonder, asked, “Bhog, sometimes I’m scared of things I don’t understand. How can I be brave?”

Bhog’s heart softened at her innocence. “Kalpana, Krishna teaches that fear comes from forgetting our true nature. You are not just this body or this mind — you are an eternal soul, connected to the divine. When you remember that, fear loses its power over you. Be brave, little one, for the divine is always with you.”

Kalpana smiled, feeling the strength of Bhog’s words within her small frame.

Ideology of Buddha

1. The Four Noble Truths

Ravi asked Bhog, "I have read a lot about Buddha, what did Buddha mean by suffering? Isn't life meant to be enjoyed?"

Bhog smiled softly and explained, "Ravi, Buddha observed that suffering (Dukkha) is inherent in life. It arises from our attachments and desires. The truth is not that life is devoid of joy, but that when we become attached to fleeting moments of happiness, we set ourselves up for suffering when those moments pass. To recognize suffering and its causes is the first step toward liberation."

Ravi nodded thoughtfully, beginning to grasp the concept of life's inherent challenges.

2. The Eightfold Path: A Guide for Living

Kartik, always striving to balance his duties and spiritual aspirations, asked, "Bhog, how can I follow Buddha's path in my daily life? I feel pulled between my responsibilities and my desire for inner peace."

Bhog replied, "Kartik, Buddha offered the Eightfold Path — a guide for how to live ethically and mindfully. You can follow this path while fulfilling your responsibilities. For example, Right Livelihood teaches us to choose work that aligns with our values. Right Speech encourages us to speak kindly, and Right Effort reminds us to put our energy into positive actions. You don't need to renounce your life; you simply need to bring mindfulness and intention to every action."

Kartik felt a deep sense of relief, realizing he could integrate spirituality into his daily routine.

3. **Mindfulness and Present Moment Awareness**

   Amara, whose creative spirit often led her to feel overwhelmed by future projects, asked, "How can I be more present, Bhog? My mind always races ahead."

   Bhog gently reminded her, "Amara, Buddha's teachings on mindfulness are about being fully present in each moment. When you create, focus entirely on the process, not the end result. When you eat, savor each bite. When you breathe, feel the air entering and leaving your body. The present moment is all we truly have — if you live in it fully, you'll find peace."

   Amara smiled, feeling inspired to bring more presence into her creative endeavors.

4. **Impermanence and Letting Go of Attachments**

   Anika, who often struggled with the loss of loved ones, asked, "Bhog, how do I find peace with the fact that everything in life seems so impermanent?"

   Bhog replied with compassion, "Anika, impermanence (Anicca) is one of the central teachings of Buddha. Everything in life is constantly changing. When we understand this deeply, we can let go of our need to hold on to people, experiences, and material things. We learn to love without attachment, knowing that change is the nature of life."

   Anika wiped a tear from her eye, feeling a sense of calm wash over her as she accepted the transient nature of life.

5. **Non-Attachment and Simplicity**

   Radha, the nurturing mother, asked, "Bhog, how can I raise my children with love but without becoming overly attached to their outcomes in life?"

Bhog's voice was gentle, "Radha, non-attachment doesn't mean you love your children any less. It means you love them with an open heart, allowing them the freedom to walk their own path. You provide them with guidance, but you do not cling to their choices or try to control their future. Buddha taught us to love without attachment — to offer our best and then let go."

Radha nodded, understanding that her role was to guide, not to control, the destinies of her children.

6. **Right Livelihood and Ethical Living**

Ravi, always energetic and ambitious, asked, "Bhog, how do I choose work that aligns with Buddha's teachings?"

Bhog looked at Ravi with admiration. "Ravi, Buddha spoke of Right Livelihood. This means choosing work that benefits others and causes no harm. Whether you are a teacher, a farmer, or an artist, what matters is that your work contributes positively to the world. When you work with integrity and mindfulness, your livelihood becomes part of your spiritual practice."

Ravi grinned, eager to find ways to align his work with his values.

7. **Compassion and Empathy**

Kalpana, the youngest in the group, asked innocently, "Bhog, how can I be kinder to others?"

Bhog's face softened, "Kalpana, kindness is one of the most powerful things we can offer the world. Buddha taught Karuna, compassion, which means feeling the suffering of others as your own. When someone hurts you, try to see their pain. When someone is kind, appreciate their heart. With practice, your empathy will grow, and you will naturally act from a place of love."

Kalpana smiled, feeling the warmth of compassion fill her small heart.

8. **Meditation and Mind Training**

   Arjun, the elder and a man of wisdom, asked, "How can we quiet the mind in a world full of distractions, Bhog?"

   Bhog's voice grew quiet and still, "Arjun, meditation is the practice that Buddha taught for quieting the mind. When you sit in silence, focusing on your breath, you train your mind to stay present. Over time, the chatter of the world fades away, and you find a stillness within that nothing can disturb. This practice, Samadhi, leads to wisdom and peace."

   Arjun nodded in agreement, knowing that meditation would be his path to deeper clarity.

9. **Generosity and Noble Friendships**

   Yash, curious as ever, asked, "Bhog, why is generosity so important in Buddha's teachings?"

   Bhog smiled warmly, "Yash, Buddha emphasized Dana, or generosity, because giving opens the heart. When we give without expecting anything in return, we feel a sense of connection to others. Generosity creates a ripple of kindness that spreads through our community. By being generous, we cultivate noble friendships — those who support us on our spiritual journey."

   Yash grinned, eager to practice generosity in his own small ways.

10. Equanimity in Life's Challenges

Arjun, reflecting on his long life, asked, "Bhog, how can we stay calm when life throws difficulties our way?"

Bhog's voice was steady as he said, "Arjun, Buddha taught Upekkha, equanimity. Life will always bring both joy and sorrow, but when we remain balanced, we can face both without losing our peace. It's about accepting that challenges are part of the human experience. When you face difficulties with a calm heart, you will find that they pass, just like everything else."

Arjun smiled, feeling the wisdom of years and the truth in Bhog's words.

As the evening deepened and the stars began to twinkle in the sky, Bhog looked around at his beloved community — each person unique in their journey yet connected by their shared quest for wisdom. He spoke softly, "The teachings of Buddha remind us that suffering is a part of life, but so is the path to liberation. By following the Eightfold Path, practicing mindfulness, and cultivating compassion, we can transform our lives and find peace."

The group sat in quiet reflection, each person feeling touched by the timeless wisdom of Buddha. They knew that these teachings would guide them through the challenges of life, helping them to live with more love, kindness, and inner calm.

As the villagers slowly rose and made their way home, the moonlight casting a gentle glow over the village, Bhog remained under the banyan tree, content that the wisdom of Buddha had found fertile ground in their hearts. The teachings of the enlightened one would continue to ripple through their lives, like a stone dropped into a still pond, spreading peace, love, and understanding throughout the world.

Ideology of Kabir

As the cool evening settled in and the villagers gathered once more under the ancient banyan tree, they found Bhog sitting in serene contemplation. The scent of blooming jasmine filled the air, and the soft murmur of the nearby river created an atmosphere of peace. Tonight, Bhog was ready to share the timeless wisdom of Kabir, a 15th-century mystic poet whose teachings bridged the gap between Hinduism and Islam, inspiring millions with his messages of unity, love, and inner reflection.

1. **Oneness of the Divine**

   Radha, always drawn to spiritual discussions, was the first to speak. "Bhog, Kabir spoke of one God, yet there are so many religions. How do we reconcile this?"

   Bhog smiled and replied, "Kabir saw beyond the divisions that humans create. He emphasized the oneness of the divine, teaching that God is formless and omnipresent, present in all things. Instead of looking outward for God in rituals or symbols, Kabir urged us to find God within ourselves. This is the key to unity among all beings."

   Radha nodded, her heart swelling with the realization that the divine resides within all, transcending religious boundaries.

2. **Simplicity and Humility**

   Kartik, who often felt the burden of societal expectations, asked, "How can we live more simply, Bhog? I feel overwhelmed by the pressures of status and material success."

Bhog's gaze softened as he responded, "Kartik, Kabir's life was one of simplicity and humility. He rejected the need for external recognition and material possessions. Kabir teaches us that true wealth lies in a humble heart and a simple life. When we let go of ego and material desires, we find inner peace."

Kartik exhaled deeply, sensing a weight lifting from his shoulders. He resolved to simplify his life and focus on what truly mattered — family, love, and self-growth.

3. **Inner Journey**

Amara, always seeking deeper meaning, leaned forward. "Bhog, Kabir often spoke of the inner journey. How do we begin this?"

Bhog's eyes sparkled with wisdom. "Amara, the path to understanding Kabir's teachings begins within. Kabir believed that true knowledge is not found in books or rituals, but in self-exploration. Meditation, silence, and self-reflection are ways to embark on this inner journey. By looking inward, you will find the answers you seek."

Amara felt a deep resonance with these words, eager to begin her own journey of inner discovery.

4. **Universal Love**

Yash, the young idealist, asked with curiosity, "Bhog, how can we love everyone equally, like Kabir taught?"

Bhog chuckled softly, "Yash, Kabir believed in universal love, a love that transcends caste, religion, and social status. To practice this, we must cultivate compassion for all beings, seeing the divine in everyone. Love freely, without judgment, and you will experience the oneness of humanity."

Yash smiled, inspired to practice compassion in his interactions with everyone, from his peers to strangers.

5. **Detachment from Worldly Attachments**

Anika, reflecting on the difficulties of family life, asked, "Bhog, how do we remain loving and caring while staying detached from worldly attachments?"

Bhog answered, "Anika, detachment does not mean withdrawing from your loved ones or responsibilities. It means loving without the need for control or ownership. Kabir teaches us to serve and care for others without becoming attached to the outcome. In doing so, we live with a full heart, yet remain free from the burdens of expectations."

Anika felt a deep sense of peace as she realized she could love her family while also releasing her need to control their lives.

6. **Inner Silence (Maun)**

Ravi, ever energetic, asked, "Bhog, how can someone like me, always active, find silence within?"

Bhog smiled at Ravi's enthusiasm. "Ravi, silence is not about inactivity. It is about quieting the mind, even when you are busy. Kabir spoke of Maun, inner silence, as the space where we connect with the divine. Practice finding stillness within, even in the midst of your activity. It will bring you clarity and peace."

Ravi nodded, eager to try moments of inner silence amidst his busy days.

7. **Truthfulness (Satya)**

Kalpana, the youngest of the group, asked innocently, "Bhog, why is telling the truth so important?"

Bhog gently responded, "Kalpana, Kabir valued Satya — truthfulness in all things. Living truthfully, in your words, thoughts, and actions, brings harmony to your life. When we are truthful, we align with the divine and build trust in our relationships."

Kalpana smiled brightly, vowing to always speak the truth, even in the smallest of moments.

8. **Service to Humanity**

Arjun, the village elder, spoke, "Bhog, I feel fulfilled when I help others. Is this the path Kabir spoke of?"

Bhog's voice was warm. "Yes, Arjun, Kabir believed that serving humanity is one of the highest forms of devotion. When we serve others selflessly, we serve God. Acts of kindness, no matter how small, are ways to express our love for the divine in every being."

Arjun smiled, knowing that his years of service had brought him closer to the divine.

9. **Devotion and Bhakti**

Radha, feeling a deep connection to Kabir's bhakti, asked, "Bhog, how can I strengthen my devotion to the divine?"

Bhog's voice was gentle as he replied, "Radha, Kabir's path of Bhakti is one of love and surrender. You can strengthen your devotion through prayer, chanting, or simply dedicating each action to the divine. Bhakti is not about rituals — it's about love. When you act from a place of love, you are in constant communion with the divine."

Radha's heart swelled with devotion, eager to express her love for the divine in every moment.

10. Equality and Social Justice

Yash, always questioning the unfairness in the world, asked, "Bhog, how did Kabir address the divisions in society?"

Bhog's tone grew serious, "Yash, Kabir was a fierce advocate for equality. He rejected caste, religious divisions, and social hierarchies, teaching that all beings are equal in the eyes of the divine. We must stand against discrimination and injustice, treating all with dignity and respect."

Yash felt inspired to work toward a world where everyone is seen as equal, regardless of their background.

Ideology of Guru Nanak

1. **Oneness with the Divine (Ik Onkar)**

   Radha, who always felt a deep connection to spiritual matters, asked, "Bhog, what did Guru Nanak mean by Ik Onkar?"

   Bhog smiled and said, "Radha, Ik Onkar is the foundation of Guru Nanak's teachings. It speaks of the oneness of the divine, that there is one God who is present in all creation. Recognizing this oneness leads us to see equality among all beings, fostering respect, compassion, and humility."

   Radha nodded, understanding that true unity comes from recognizing the divinity in everyone and everything.

2. **Honest Living (Kirat Karni)**

Kartik, always focused on his responsibilities, asked, "How can we apply Guru Nanak's teaching of earning an honest living?"

Bhog replied, "Kartik, Kirat Karni means working with integrity and earning through righteous means. It's about living honestly and using your skills and efforts to contribute to society. When you live with integrity, you not only earn wealth but also moral fulfillment."

Kartik felt a sense of pride in his work, knowing that by living ethically, he was honoring Guru Nanak's teachings.

3. **Sharing and Generosity (Vand Chakna)**

Amara, who often felt the urge to give back, asked, "Bhog, how can we truly live by Vand Chakna, the principle of sharing?"

Bhog's face lit up, "Amara, Vand Chakna is the practice of sharing what you have, whether it is wealth, time, or compassion. It is about cultivating a generous spirit and creating a sense of community. When we share, we not only help others but also build bonds of love and unity."

Amara felt the warmth of these words, eager to share her blessings with those in need.

4. **Naam Japna (Chanting the Divine Name)**

Yash, ever curious about spirituality, asked, "Bhog, how can we connect with the divine like Guru Nanak taught?"

Bhog gently responded, "Yash, Naam Japna is the constant remembrance of God. It can be through chanting, prayer, or meditation. By making time for daily spiritual practice, we connect more deeply with the divine and cultivate inner peace."

Yash felt inspired to incorporate chanting and meditation into his daily life, seeking a deeper spiritual connection.

5. **Equality and Social Justice (Sarbat da Bhala)**

Ravi, passionate about justice, asked, "Bhog, Guru Nanak fought against inequality. How can we apply his teachings today?"

Bhog nodded, "Ravi, Guru Nanak believed in Sarbat da Bhala, or the well-being of all. He rejected the caste system and taught that everyone, regardless of gender, religion, or status, is equal. In our lives, we can stand up for equality and work for social justice, ensuring that everyone is treated with dignity and respect."

Ravi felt energized, knowing that he could contribute to a more just and equal world.

6. **Humility (Nimrata)**

Kalpana, with her innocence, asked, "Bhog, why is humility so important?"

Bhog answered softly, "Kalpana, humility or Nimrata is about recognizing that we are all part of something greater. Guru Nanak taught that true greatness comes from humility, as it allows us to see the divine in others and live with kindness."

Kalpana smiled, understanding that humility was a virtue that brought people closer together in love.

7. **Compassion (Daya)**

Anika, always sensitive to the needs of others, asked, "Bhog, how can we practice compassion like Guru Nanak taught?"

Bhog replied, "Anika, Daya or compassion is about extending love and understanding to all beings. It means being sensitive to the suffering of others and acting with kindness. Compassion is not just a feeling, it's an action — helping those in need, offering comfort, and showing empathy."

Anika felt her heart soften, realizing that compassion is an essential part of her spiritual journey.

8. **Contentment (Santokh)**

Arjun, who had seen the many phases of life, asked, "Bhog, how can we be content in a world that constantly pushes us to want more?"

Bhog's voice was calm. "Arjun, Santokh or contentment is about appreciating what we have and recognizing that true happiness comes from within. Guru Nanak taught that when we are content with what life gives us, we free ourselves from the endless pursuit of material desires and find peace in the present."

Arjun smiled, knowing that his contentment would bring him closer to spiritual fulfillment.

9. **Selfless Service (Seva)**

Radha, inspired by Guru Nanak's message, asked, "Bhog, how can we make Seva, or selfless service, a part of our lives?"

Bhog's face softened, "Radha, Seva is about serving others without expecting anything in return. It could be helping a neighbor, volunteering, or simply offering a kind word. Selfless service connects us to the divine, as we see God in those we serve."

Radha felt her heart swell with gratitude, eager to engage in more acts of selfless service.

10. Living Truthfully (Sat)

Yash, ever focused on honesty, asked, "Bhog, what does it mean to live truthfully?"

Bhog smiled, "Yash, Sat means living in alignment with the truth — being honest with yourself and others. It is about following the path of righteousness, even when it is difficult. When we live truthfully, we embody Guru Nanak's teachings and create harmony in our lives."

Yash felt a deep sense of purpose, ready to live with more integrity in every action.

11. Detachment from Materialism (Vairag)

Kartik, who often struggled with balancing work and spiritual life, asked, "Bhog, how can we let go of material attachments while still living in the world?"

Bhog answered with a gentle smile, "Kartik, Vairag means detachment from materialism, but it doesn't mean rejecting the world. It means finding spiritual fulfillment beyond possessions and valuing relationships and experiences over things. By practicing detachment, we realize that true joy comes from within."

Kartik felt a wave of relief, understanding that detachment was about finding balance and inner peace.

12. Environmental Stewardship

Ravi, a lover of nature, asked, “Bhog, how did Guru Nanak view nature?”

Bhog’s eyes gleamed with understanding. “Ravi, Guru Nanak believed in the sanctity of nature. He saw the divine presence in the environment and taught that we must respect and care for the earth. Practicing environmental stewardship involves living sustainably and ensuring that we protect the world for future generations.”

Ravi felt a renewed sense of responsibility to care for the earth and promote sustainability.

As the stars began to twinkle overhead, Bhog looked at the villagers gathered around him, their faces illuminated by the gentle glow of lanterns. He knew that Guru Nanak’s teachings had resonated deeply with each one of them. “Guru Nanak’s wisdom is not just to be admired — it is to be lived. His message of oneness, humility, and service offers a path to inner peace and a more just and compassionate world. By embodying these values in our daily lives, we honor the divine presence within and around us.”

The villagers rose, each carrying with them a piece of Guru Nanak’s teachings in their hearts. As they walked back to their homes, the night felt peaceful, filled with the promise of living truthfully, compassionately, and with devotion to the oneness of all beings.

As Bhog concluded his illuminating discourse, the once-bustling village now echoed with a profound stillness. The audience sat in contemplative silence, each heart touched and inspired by the timeless wisdom shared by the venerable.

Bhog, with a serene gaze and a gentle smile, addressed the gathered community, “Dear friends, in the tapestry of these timeless teachings, we find the essence of what it means to lead a life of purpose, compassion, and spiritual awakening. As we navigate the currents of existence, let us draw upon the teachings of Ashtavakra, Krishna, Guru Nanak, Kabir, and Buddha as guiding stars."

He continued, "May the self-realization of Ashtavakra guide you to transcend the limitations of the mind and discover the boundless truth within. Embrace the wisdom of Krishna to navigate the complexities of life with righteous action and unwavering duty."

Bhog's eyes sparkled with the light of wisdom as he spoke further, "Guru Nanak's message of oneness and equality should resonate in our hearts, encouraging us to see the divinity in all beings. The mystical verses of Kabir remind us to unravel the illusions of the material world and seek the essence that connects us all."

A gentle breeze swept through the village as Bhog shared his concluding words, "In the footsteps of Buddha, may we cultivate compassion and mindfulness. As the stories of these great sages echo in our hearts, let us embark on a journey of self-discovery and transformation."

As the retreat drew to a close, Bhog gathered everyone one last time beneath the ancient trees where their journey had begun. His voice, calm yet filled with purpose, echoed the timeless wisdom they had explored together. "The path of understanding never truly ends," he said, looking into the eyes of each seeker. "What we have learned here is but the beginning. Life will continue to present its lessons, and it is in those moments that you will find the true meaning of these teachings."

The group, filled with gratitude, knew that this was not a farewell but a pause before the next step of the journey. Bhog had not only shared knowledge but created a space for inner transformation — one that would stay with them as they returned to their daily lives.

As the days of the retreat came to an end, there was a shared sense of anticipation for the next gathering, when they would return to Bhog's guidance to delve deeper into life's mysteries. The wisdom they had gained here would be a foundation for future retreats, where new insights and deeper truths awaited.

With hearts full of appreciation for all that Bhog had offered, the group knew that this was not an end, but a continuation—each of them carrying a piece of the retreat with them, ready to return when the call for further discovery arose.

Disclaimer:

The content in this book, *"Breath of Sages,"* is intended for informational and educational purposes only. The teachings, interpretations, and insights provided are based on spiritual concepts and are meant to inspire personal reflection and growth. Readers are encouraged to approach the material with an open mind, while also considering their unique experiences and beliefs.

The views expressed in this book reflect the author's interpretations and should not be considered definitive representations of any specific spiritual tradition or philosophy. They are intended to foster understanding and inner exploration, and not to prescribe any particular religious or spiritual practices.

All images are AI-generated and intended for illustrative purposes only and should not be considered exact representations of any real-world individuals, locations, or events.

The author and publisher disclaim any responsibility for any personal or societal outcomes resulting from the application of the ideas or practices discussed in the book. Readers are encouraged to seek guidance from qualified professionals or spiritual mentors when necessary.

www.ingramcontent.com/pod-product-compliance
Lightning Source LLC
LaVergne TN
LVHW041201150826
845673LV00001B/253